Kiss Ma Bell Good-bye

REVISED AND UPDATED EDITION ✳

Kiss Ma Bell Good-bye

How to Install

Your Own

Telephones,

Extensions, Accessories—

& Save Lots of Money

Wesley Cox

**author of CRIME STOPPERS
and ENERGY SMARTS**

CROWN PUBLISHERS, INC., NEW YORK

Author's note: All the suggestions and processes described in this book are designed to be completed legally and pleasurably by any prudent person, young or old.

The Communications Act of 1934 in the United States was amended January 8, 1982, making these activities legal. In Canada, comparable legislation was enacted on the advice of the nation's Supreme Court.

This book is designed to make telephone service a practical and enjoyable activity.

Published by Crown Publishers, Inc., One Park Avenue, New York, New York 10016, and simultaneously in Canada by General Publishing Company Limited

Manufactured in the United States of America

CROWN is a trademark of Crown Publishers, Inc.

LIBRARY OF CONGRESS CATALOGING IN PUBLICATION DATA

Cox, Wesley.
   Kiss Ma Bell good-bye.

   Includes index.
   1. Telephone—Amateurs' manuals. I. Title.
TK9951.C68 1985   621.386   85-5722
ISBN 0-517-55840-8

Illustrations by James Barry

10 9 8 7 6 5 4 3 2 1

First Revised and Updated Edition

Dedicated to Alva,
who knows why

CONTENTS

PART FOUR—*An Inside Look at Things Present and Future*

APPENDICES

LIST OF FIGURES

With appreciation to Bud Ball,
who provided the technical assurance
that everything described in this book
will work as promised.
Having spent three decades working with Ma,
he ought to know.

PREFACE

The largest corporation in the world lost the World Series of Big Business on January 8, 1982.

MA BELL WAS CLOBBERED

It had taken a century from Alexander Graham Bell's patent on the telephone, March 7, 1876, for American ingenuity to build that single device into American Telephone and Telegraph, Inc. (AT&T), the biggest and maybe the best conglomerate on planet Earth. Familiarly known as Ma Bell, she'd built up a $150 *billion* net worth of communications facilities, too immense to comprehend.

For the sake of understanding, Ma had shuffled her huge squad into twenty-three separate operating companies and in every sense was the country's original "Big Leaguer."

She used the money of a few million backers and the brains and muscles of a million workers to get the job done. There were a few big independent teams that never challenged Ma. GTE and Continental were two of a dozen or more, all of them in the Big Leagues, like Ma, but lacking her immensity. She retained the Biggest Business pennant for ten decades.

Then too, there was a Little League of a few thousand Mom and Pop telephone systems, really out in the boondocks, too small for Ma to worry about. She'd take their money for providing long-distance service for the local customers who wanted to call out of town. If they went broke or agreed to sell out cheap, Ma bought them.

Ma built all her own equipment, too, with her Western Electric homemade subsidiary. And she sold or rented everything and anything that would make a buck. Ma stayed ahead of everybody's game plans, doing research that nobody else could afford, through her own Bell Labs. They'd pay their way selling inventions and taking royalties on fantastic things like transistors, touch dialers, and defense devices for her old buddy the Pentagon, and anybody else with lots of money to spend.

She was both a saint and a sinner. Ma threw more curves at more people and smaller businesses than Tom Seaver at his best. And every time she was called to bat, she'd wham a homer.

BIGGER THAN BIG GOVERNMENT

Ma Bell would do anything to make a fast score and was never afraid to slug for it. That's what scared Big Government when they saw she was getting as big as they were. Government played hardball too, but they liked to win all their games with as little sweat as possible. Both Ma and Big G wanted to play the game, but they liked the idea of owning all the bats, balls, and players, and the ballpark, too. Big Government started tossing curves at Ma. Her first error may have been the "Consent Decree"—a new game rule to which she was pressured by the lawyers in '56. In effect, the decree enabled Ma to keep her monopoly, on condition that she wouldn't get into any business other than telephones. For Ma it was Strike One!

WHIFFED AGAIN

Thirteen years later, an upstart called MCI (Microwave Communications, Inc.) got an okay from the FCC (Federal Communications Commission) to transmit phone calls through the air between St. Louis and Chicago. An even smaller outfit, Carterfone, had used the courts to snatch a crumb of Ma Bell's action years earlier, but it had been too insignificant to worry about, it seemed. A bunt, at best. In retrospect, Carterfone's success gave MCI the incentive to get into the game. MCI's big hit was Ma's second strike. Ma kept working. She was the biggest and the best. Everybody knew it. Why worry?

WEEP NO TEARS FOR DEAR OLD MA

She hung in there, making home runs, getting bigger, big enough to make the Big G's Justice Department send their lawyers out with an antitrust suit against AT&T in 1974. Their gambit was that Ma was freezing out all competition. Is there any major corporation that doesn't try the same tactic? But after seven years of swinging, running, and hitting, Ma Bell struck out. The antitrust action was over. She'd used the years of legal shenanigans to plan an invasion of the computer market and other office equipment businesses, anyway. Ma might lose an inning but never a game! When the right moment came, Ma whiffed her third strike and accepted an "out."

MA'S DAY OF RECKONING

On January 8, 1982, Ma said, "Okay, guys. We give up our monopoly, but be warned, we're staying in the game, not only for telephones, but everything else we can do well."

The assets of Ma Bell were refinanced and restructured as *seven* regional companies. Was Ma dead? No chance. Ma had given up only the farm teams. When, on January 1, 1984, she gave up ownership of the regional operating companies (soon to be renamed the Seven Sisters), she launched her new strategy. As we know now, Ma was always thinking ahead, and fast on her feet. She plays to WIN and don't you forget it!

AFTER THE "DIVESTITURE"

Ma Bell, with court approval, maintains her AT&T Communications Division, basically the big money-maker, long distance, by wire, microwave, satellite, and clout. Her second Division is a new World Series. In it, the AT&T Technologies groups direct Ma's Information Systems (her old phone service, revised), AT&T Labs (research as usual), Network Systems (Western Electric as before), International (Ma's invading the world with all her services), and two new kids, AT&T Consumer Products (making everything from phones to computers) and AT&T Technology (making the parts to build the equipment, from computer chips to circuit boards). Gangway! Here comes Ma Bell, richer, rougher, tougher, meaner, and leaner than ever before. Nobody but nobody messes with Ma Bell.

MEANWHILE, BACK AT YOUR PHONE . . .

The lawyers had settled back to count their money, leaving the managers and technicians to feel the chill of being orphans. Unless you were and still remain with one of the *big* independents, like GTE, Rochester, Continental, or one of a dozen others, or any of the multitude of sandlot systems, you'll be getting bills from your same old firm, now merged into one of the new groups. The bills, like the groups, will be bigger.

The new regional groups, comprised of former local companies, became Bell Atlantic, NYNEX, U.S. West, Ameritech, Southwestern Bell, Pacific Telesis, and Bell South. Canada Bell, which was always a bastard stepchild, would remain much the same as before. These regional umbrellas would provide their local outfits with technical and support service, help them develop and market mobile equipment, and be cheerleaders for the same, original local companies, which would provide local dial tone service, sell products, and publish directories. Instead of *one* gigantic confection, it was a mixed bag of ballpark peanuts, that was all. Ma Bell was benched, briefly. She just doesn't own the whole game anymore. But she's happy! Ma is planning to get into an even bigger game, if you want to know the truth. She's ready to compete against all comers.

AND YOU, TOO, ARE DEREGULATED

You, dear reader, may wonder why Ma's dandy phone system was dumped when she seemed to be doing so great out there in the field. Will the new system be as good as the old? Will the costs rise or fall? First: Divestiture was made in the name of preserving competitive private enterprise. As for the other questions, your guess is as good as anybody's, including that of Charlie Brown, the Big Boss of new AT&T. The local companies and/or regional operations still have some roadwork to do. They're still fiddling with their game plan, tinkering with switches, most of them seeking *billions* of dollars in increased rates, out of your pockets.

They feel the awesome presence of Ma Bell without having her fantastic coaching and cash to count on. They're being pressed by new manufacturers. They're trying to learn what the world of competition is all about. They're trying every trick imaginable (the lawyers need something to do again) to confuse your monthly bills, calling zones, and service. Things are almost bound to get worse before they get immensely better.

Is there any certain answer for you, just you, right now?

HELP IS IN YOUR HAND, MY FRIEND

Yes, there are three self-serving things that you should do to protect yourself and your phone service, probably the most convenient of all your utilities. The sooner, the better.

1. Buy your own equipment and stop renting from Ma or her offspring. Pay only your monthly "basic service" and go looking for the lowest possible long-distance charges.

2. Join a Citizens Action Group to counterattack the company lawyers seeking to raise your phone rates sky-high. Don't picket your local phone company. Meet with your neighbors and take a sneaky lawyer to lunch. Let him or her do battle with the phone company's SWAT teams. And finally . . .

3. Learn how simple it is to install and maintain your own in-house or small office phone system.

You can *Kiss Ma Bell Good-bye*, without fear of trauma.

This book tells you how to do it all.

Try it, you'll like it—after the first shock of doing your own thing without Ma Bell's strategies.

INTRODUCTION

MISTER BELL'S TELEPHONE—THE TRUE STORY

. . . for readers with romance in their hearts!

This book is really a step-by-step description to enable anyone, no matter how inept, fumble-fingered, or scared, to save hundreds of dollars doing his or her own telephone installation, now that Ma Bell has moved on to other activities. If you want to jump instantly into the action, skip on to page 19. But if you miss the next few pages, you'll miss some of the knowledge and much of the drama in the telephone business you're entering.

The Ma Bell story has more pathos than a decade of phony soap opera. And every word of it is true; no sugar or spice, not even adultery, has been added to jazz it up!

FADE IN

Electric lighting systems, horseless carriages, central heating, and short-distance telegraphy were barely under way when Alexander Graham Bell was born March 3, 1847, in Edinburgh, Scotland. His mother, Elisa Grace Symonds, painted portraits and was an accomplished musician. His father, Alexander Melville Bell, had developed a system of symbols and used them for the purpose of teaching deaf-mutes to speak. Can't you just picture the agonies and ecstasies of getting into that kind of business?

Young Alexander was named for his grandfather, a teacher of good speech practices who also gave dramatic readings from Shakespeare.

ALEXANDER TRIES OUT THE WORLD'S BIGGEST IDEA

Out of this background of interes in communications and enrollment as a teacher-student at Weston House, a boys' school near Edinburgh, in company with his two brothers, Alexander Graham Bell became fascinated with the notion of perhaps "telegraphing" speech. Don't miss this part of the story — it makes modern fiction sound like cold potatoes.

A host of brilliant minds had been toying with electrical eye-openers since 600 B.C., when Greek philosopher Thales of Miletus found that by rubbing amber with cloth, the amber could be made to attract feathers and balls of wool. An English doctor named William Gilbert documented centuries of Middle Ages magnetic/electrical oddities with his book, written in 1600.

The 1700s saw Gray in England, Du Fay in France, and Ben Franklin in America, with many others, missing meals and skipping parties, wine, women, and song, to advance the thing we call electricity.

LIGHT ON THE SUBJECT

The next century saw Italy's Galvani and Volta, Denmark's Oersted, France's Ampère, Germany's Ohm and Seebeck push our knowledge of electrical/magnetic forces toward common usage. About the time the Bell family was shaping up, England's Michael Faraday and America's Joseph Henry were agonizing over electrical-generation procedures. James Maxwell, a Scot, was straining over laws governing their findings, and Germany's Heinrich Hertz was noodling around with radio waves.

These gentlemen were brilliant doodlers, inventors in the raw. One individual, Nikola Tesla, born in 1856 in Smiljan, Austro-Hungary (now Yugoslavia), was the most likely "perfect genius," who methodically, scientifically, with disciplined passion, developed the ultimate electric motor, arc lighting, extraordinary magnifying transmitters, and incredible new electromechanical devices even while moving from home to Czechoslovakia, France, and the United States, where his motors brought fame and celebrity to the Westinghouse Company.

I can assure you, here and now, there's more true romance to be found in the stories of electrons than you'll get in a year of reading the supermarket tabloids. Family involvements, intense excitements, investor enthusiasms, jealousies, hates, divorces and marriages were played out relentlessly through the discovery process, almost in anticipation of a resolver, a catalyst, a bringer-together of imagination and science, a knight in shining armor. It would be Alexander Graham Bell, student of voice, dabbler in electrical matters, a sloppy benchworker, who would bring it all together, though not without heartrending hardship and disappointment. The story has more twists and turns than a Judith Krantz novel. For example . . .

Because of the premature deaths, caused by tuberculosis, of his oldest and youngest sons, Bell's father felt hexed. When he was advised that Alexander almost certainly had "consumption," Dad Bell abandoned his career. Flat out. He packed up and skipped, taking his loved ones with him. He moved the family first to London, England, thence to Brantford, Ontario, Canada. There, young Alexander recovered from the life-threatening disease and plunged into a dedication of interlocking his knowledge of speech with the new science of electrical energy. It was rough going. Money was scarce, and there was no unemployment compensation in those days.

ON THE ROAD AGAIN

To support himself, he accepted a teaching job at Boston University, instructing the deaf, among them Mabel Hubbard, the daughter of a local attorney. Miss Hubbard and Alexander began "seeing each other." Another association developed with Tom Sanders, a Boston merchant who joined with his pal, Miss Hubbard's father, to finance Bell's experiments. Some way to marry off a handicapped daughter, eh? Truthfully, Dad's intentions were quite honorable. Yet everybody, including Bell himself, sensed the moneymaking possibilities in this notion that there should be better ways to communicate than nose to nose or by Sam Morse's code, which had been dot-dashing around since 1837. Dozens, if not hundreds, of brains were toiling with the same possibilities and frustrations, all over the planet. It was a great idea to talk to other people, back and forth, over a wire, probably with a shot of electricity behind it. Who would get to the goal first? That was the big question! This author is convinced it would have been Tesla, the Disciplined, if he hadn't been engrossed in motors. Would we have wound up using Teslaphones? Later it would be revealed that a vast number of inventors were reaching the same points of discovery almost synchronously with Alexander Graham Bell.

Can you sense the drama in this sequence of events? You won't find anything as gripping on *General Hospital, Edge of Night,* or *As the World Turns,* believe me. And *this* is true!

HE NEEDS MR. WATSON

Bell's advance money led him to a machine shop, where another relative youngster, Tom Watson, agreed to help. After vast numbers of failing experiments, voice over wire, a gimmick worked. On June 2, 1875, Watson accidentally plucked a reed and the sound was heard, carried by wire into the next room, where Bell was working away at another shot-in-the-dark device.

Bell rushed into Watson's workshop, crying, "Watson, what did you do? Change nothing. Let me see what you did."

In the next instant, Bell's genius grasped the process. He dictated to Watson the requirements for constructing the first telephone. Next day, the overnight device transmitted Bell's voice, unintelligible but unmistakable, to Watson, by means of electrical impulses over wires.

The telephone was invented! Well, almost. Unaware of the worldwide competition, our heroes tinkered and toiled to improve their happenstantial success.

GAMES INVENTORS PLAY

After experimenting through the summer, Bell applied for a patent in September of 1875. It was granted March 7, 1876. Three days later, when Bell and Watson were experimenting in different rooms, Bell sloshed some battery acid on the equipment and also on his clothing. The acid burned the cloth and started sizzling Alexander's hide. It was then that he called the now-famous words, "Mister Watson, come here. I need you." The voice transmission and reception were loud and clear, most importantly, over the wire!

The newly invented telephone had undergone its first improvement, in a process that continues to this day. And that "perfection by accident" unleashed the Bell concept, the Bell system, soon renamed the Bell Telephone Company (July 9, 1877).

THE ROGUES RETURN

As rodents smell cheese, lawyers smell money. Bogus suits to swipe Bell's success were filed within days of that first "hello." Alexander Graham kissed them off, married Mabel, and took the next boat for England, leaving his affairs in the trustworthy hands of Tom Watson.

Some bozos did a few end runs around the newly formed Bell Company, setting up independent companies with little regard for Bell's patents. One of the heavyweight groups, incorporated in 1885 as American Telephone and Telegraph Company, made an open and acceptable deal with the Bell Company people to go out for a sea-to-sea system of telephone service.

By 1899, AT&T, as it soon became known, was in firm command of all Bell Telephone Company affairs. It wasn't long before AT&T became known as Ma Bell. If you had invested $50 in it back then, you'd be a multimillionaire today. Also, you'd be about 140 years old!

ONLY IN AMERICA?

Less than a hundred years later, Ma Bell was the biggest single company on planet Earth. She took over territories and installed new phone systems where none existed. If she came across an area where locals had already set up systems of their own, she bought them out, cheap—though there were hundreds of small holdouts. There still are, today. But after all, what if you wanted to make a call out of town? Deals were made to tie independents into Ma's long-distance system. Thus began AT&T's Long Lines Division.

By the time Alexander Graham Bell hung up his phone for the last time in 1922, he'd used his millions to finance other experiments of value to mankind—a myriad of activities from airplanes to piano playing, from phonograph recordings to encouraging sheep to give birth to more than one lamb at a time. He'd won enough awards and honors to cram a sizable museum in Baddeck, Nova Scotia, where he'd spent the good weather of his golden years.

THE BUSINESS OF AMERICA IS—BUSINESS

AT&T owned the telephone business, lock, stock, and ringer. Its Western Electric Division made the instruments and switches. Its Laboratory invented things that no other inventors could possibly afford to research. Its Long Lines division shuffled calls all over the continent and moved them into the global system (ITT, no forthright relation), for a fee. That's another story. Two brothers named Behn had swiped the AT&T technique and sold it, country by country, after making a deal with AT&T to stay out of North America if AT&T would give them the world. Of course, they'd buy equipment from AT&T. Although they stayed out of the phone business in the United States, ITT had the smarts to buy more than a thousand subsidiaries and subcompanies, from cookie manufacturers to car rentals. Ma Bell (AT&T) stuck to the job of telephones.

GROW, GROW, GROW YOUR BOAT

Ma Bell was so big after World War II as to be beyond belief or understanding. Also, all other companies were locked out of the telephone business because of Ma Bell's tight hold, her monopoly through multiple subcompanies, all in the phone business, with virtually no competitors. In the mid-sixties, the Justice Department said, "Hey, you guys, you're getting bigger than the government. If you don't mind, knock it off. Let somebody else into the telephone game." (ITT had anticipated problems with the Justice Department in the United States, but after all, they were doing most of their business out of town—in Hitler's Germany and Allende's Chile, to name only two. When their own antitrust suit was pressed, it faded quickly.)

These Washington intrusions are noted here because all of the super-corporations maintain super-staffs at that center of political power. When an assemblyman says "Frog," Fortune 500's companies *jump*. And also, sometimes, vice versa. AT&T

11

accepted its antitrust suit without blinking an eye. They'd seen it coming. They'd been preparing for it. All that remained was to stall for time.

HERE THEY GO AGAIN!

Just as they'd done after Alexander Graham Bell had invented the telephone, the lawyers moved in for every dollar they could grab. For seven years they fought each other, services available to the highest bidder.

On January 8, 1982, Ma Bell threw her hands in the air and said, "I surrender." Justice Department lawyers—1, Ma Bell's lawyers—0. Actually, Ma was the victor.

Remember—she'd won time enough to work out a whole new scheme. She had grown weary, anyway, of using much of her huge profits from long distance to subsidize the losses of many of her "little" businesses. And she wanted to move into new territories, like computers, other business machines. She gave up nothing but her losers. She hung on to her money-makers, like Western Electric, Long Lines, and Bell Labs, and agreed to reorganize by taking a "hands off" attitude to the local companies. Ma Bell knew from Day One she couldn't lose! So she agreed to the process called divestiture!

MA BELL RIDES AGAIN! A NEW HORSE, THAT'S ALL!

Overnight, people were jumping into the making of telephones, switches, and other gear. In addition to their own domestic products, high-quality equipment flowed into the United States and Canada from Germany, Japan, other nations—even Sri Lanka, remember it? And so too came the junk! One thing about Ma, she'd never produced many second-class products.

But divestiture meant deregulation. Like show business, anybody could get into the act. People could now install their own telephones, accessories, and other gadgets, cautioned only that they better not hook up anything that could screw up the service to the quarter of a billion other phones along the lines in the United States and Canada.

1982, '83, and '84 were horrid years for Ma Bell's customers, shareholders, and employees. Virtually run by lawyers on a day-

12

to-day basis her local companies weren't too sure what to do. As you'll see, her twenty-three companies became seven in the U.S. It remained virtually unchanged in Canada. Shareholders in AT&T could swap, trade, or do all manner of things, and tons of money flowed into AT&T's vaults. But it flowed outward faster than usual and Ma realized the whole impact of no longer owning all the ball teams, bats, balls, gloves, umpires, and the ballpark, too! She'd have to get into the game to play, to win. She had to compete! Rats!

SURPRISE? NOT LIKELY!

The old girl might have gagged a bit at the thought, but she didn't miss a heartbeat. She even bought herself a new house in '84. The AT&T headquarters just completed in New York is surely among the most expensive, luxurious, if not unbelievable, buildings in the history of mankind. Her A-Team is living in resplendent, opulent, awesome quarters.

In the meantime, Ma's own overachievers are out there gutter-fighting with all comers and doing a mighty good job of protecting the status quo. Where, once upon a time, there was one major supplier of phones and other telephone accessories, owned and leased out by Ma, there are now, as of 1985, more than 6,500 manufacturers, leasing companies, and sales operations for telephone service located in North America.

Ma's twenty-three local companies are shaking themselves down into seven independent operating units. Most are doing as well as or better than their 1981 counterparts. There are at least twenty other independent systems of substantial size scattered over the land. There are hundreds of very small and corporate-owned systems in use, using microwave dishes and satellites for interconnects. Ma doesn't have to worry much because she's got the Big Bucks stashed away from a hundred years of owning the whole thing. But Ma is a mite vulnerable in one spot where she was once invincible—long distance!

HITTING MA WHERE SHE CAN HURT

There are at least 400 long-distance suppliers nudging their way into AT&T's monopoly. Many die aborning. Eight of the

13

biggest are nibbling away at AT&T's list of 86 million customers. The big roller, the one that really started the whole telephone revolution, MCI (following the Carterfone decision, a
wrist slap of decades past), has already captured 2 million. (See
Chapter 10.) Ma is zapping away at the competition, and she's
proving she's no slouch at do-or-die economics.

Telephone customers everywhere are opening their monthly
bills and shrieking at the increase in basic rates, toll charges,
and long distance. Without subsidization from dear old Ma, the
companies are socking it to the customers. It's hard to find out
who to blame. At least you've got lots of choices.

HELP IS IN YOUR OWN HANDS

Your one and certain protection is to get into the telephone
business yourself. You *can* wire your own phones. You *can* unload the relentless monthly rental charges for equipment. And
you can readily do your own repairs if your own phones break
down. The answers are in this book.

If you think the changeover from Ma Bell to divestiture has
been a mind-boggling experience to date, be warned. You ain't
seen nothin' yet! The revolution is barely under way. The telecommunications process, gigantic as it may seem thus far, may
have taken the equivalent of five or six steps in a ten-kilometer
run. Between now and the time you stop hearing all the hoopla
for good, you're going to see and hear things on the telephone
that no human being has yet dreamed of. The ones already here
and on the drawing board are fantastic in themselves. Like it or
not, telecommunications from now into the next century are
going to change your life.

And there's only one thing about the whole mess of which
you can be positively sure. You can *Kiss Ma Bell Good-bye* but
one way or another, she's gonna fight to win you back. She
wants the money!

UPON REFLECTION

Well, what do you think? Is not this tiny peep into the Phone
Show like a chunk of soap opera? Think of the millions of people
involved. Twelve thousand AT&T employees have already been

released from their jobs. Hundreds of thousands more employees within local units can see their jobs being taken over by electronic switches and robots. Families are being uprooted in search of employment in other communities, other fields. And yet new jobs are being created within the awesome high technology. We didn't promise you a rose garden. We did promise you a practical solution to present and future problems with your own residential phone service. It starts on the very next page!

PART ONE

Telephones and Extensions

1 THE NEW SYSTEM— BASED ON THE OLD PROCESS

The new ways of doing telephone business permit you, in most communities, to wire your home, own your own phones and accessories, as you desire. Just don't do anything that will mess things up at your nearest central office. Then, hooking into Ma Bell's vast network—the product of nearly one hundred years of work involving many thousands of professionals and many millions of dollars—means nothing more or less than learning *how to tie together two wires*. Everything, but *everything*, in this gigantic system of voice communication begins and ends with *two tiny wires*. There's no danger in handling telephone wires unless an individual is very fragile. The voltage involved might sound ominous, but the current flow can best be likened to that in a household flashlight.

Let's get used to the notion of two wires and how they work to keep all of us hooked up together. Every phone needs two wires; if there were only two phones in the world they'd look like figure 1. The phone in Jones's house is connected to the phone in Smith's place by the two wires. A total of four connections, right?

Now, let's look at figure 2 to see what happens if there are a total of *five* families who might want to talk back and forth to each other. If everybody in the system is going to be able to call everyone else, it looks as though there'll have to be a couple of wires *from* everyone *to* everyone else. Four pairs of wires going "in" and "out" of each location could do it. That would total forty ($2 \times 4 \times 5$) connections, to say nothing of some kind of signal circuit and switches.

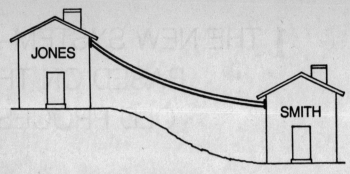

1 / TWO WIRES IT TAKES TWO TO TELEPHONE

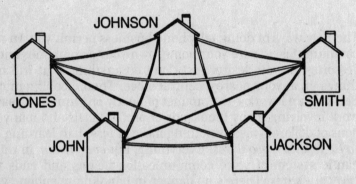

2 / FIVE HOUSES FIRST SIGNS OF A DILEMMA

Things are getting a bit messy, aren't they? And still only five telephone subscribers! That's what the telephone pioneers thought. There had to be a better way of getting things done. Ma Bell figured out a better system, fast. Skip all the wiring between each pair of houses and simply connect each location to a central office, where calls could be cross-connected or "switched" to one another. (See figure 3.) In this way, any two subscribers with wires to the central office could be connected.

Let central do the switching! Even if Jones wants to talk to his nearest neighbor, Smith, it's lots easier to send the call scooting into the central office to be switched onto Smith's line than to try laying out dozens of pairs of wires as we saw in figure 2.

And hello! What's this?

If the system works between a house and a central office, why not do exactly the same thing between central offices in

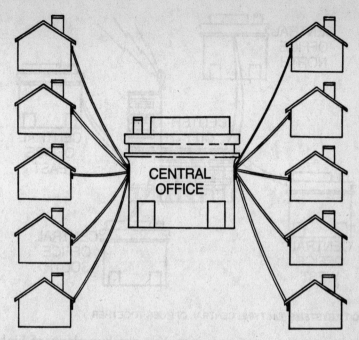

3 / CENTRAL OFFICE MA BELL MAKES HER FIRST MOVE

different parts of the city? (See figure 4.) Nifty? You bet. And exactly the same technique links cities, small towns, and unincorporated areas—by wires, by microwaves, or by bouncing the signals back and forth to satellites in outer space. (See figure 5.)

You and I benefit from all these neat inventions and networks. But the simple fact underlying the whole incredible process is that two tiny wires connect your place to your nearest central office. And those wires are yours. They've been given a number. Your telephone number. And that's all that you have to be concerned about in setting yourself up today—right now, as a budding telephone installer.

You can begin earning back the cost of this book this minute by marching your present telephone (s) back to your local telephone store and plugging in one or more of your own. Right now you are probably renting those phones from Ma and she's picking up any amount from $1.50 to $5 or more, per set per month. That's anywhere from $18 to perhaps $100·you're

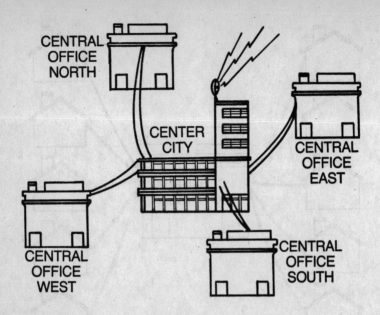

spending on every set each year. You can buy plenty of high-quality telephones for that kind of money and get the warm glow of seeing your phone bill reduced every month. You stop paying Ma a monthly phone rental when you take hers back. She'll polish it up a bit and probably rent or sell it to somebody else. Meanwhile, you'll have plugged in your own, bought from Ma or someone else.

But let's keep thinking about those two simple wires that make everything work. Whether you're calling the corner store or calling around the world, everything begins and ends with those two tiny wires. They connect your place with your nearest central office, where all the magic switching takes place. The person you're calling has a couple of wires connecting his or her phone to a central office too. Everything else in between is shared by everybody who has a telephone, an estimated 750 million of us globally. Maybe a billion—nobody's counting anymore.

Say your number is 213-555-4699 and you want to dial a friend in Tokyo. His number is 555-2702, area code 3, in Japan, which has country code 81.

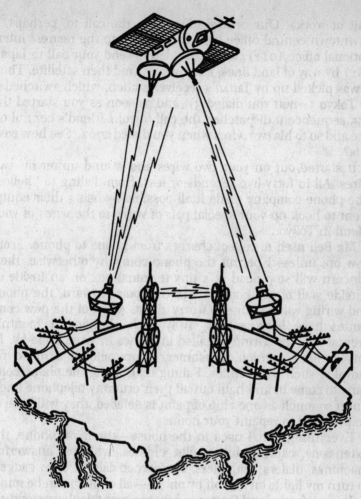

5 / CONTINENTAL SERVICE HOW LONG DISTANCE WORKS

So, in most telephone systems, you must first dial 1—that wakes up the computer at your central office and alerts it that "There's a direct-dial coming." Next you dial 011 (the international access code), followed by 81 (Japan), followed by 3 (Tokyo), and last your pal's number, 555-2702. Go slowly. Follow the sequence.

Okay. The two wires from your house carried those codes to your central office (where the computer noted it was your circuit at work). Our central office shot the call to, perhaps, a downtown central office, which relayed it to the nearest international office (011), which decided to send your call to Japan (81) by way of land lines, microwaves, and then satellite. Then it was picked up by Japan's receiver station, which switched it to Tokyo (when you dialed 3), and as soon as you started the 555 sequence it dispatched the call to your friend's central office and so to his two wires when you dialed 2702. See how easy it is?

It started out on your two wires and wound up on his two wires. All in forty-five seconds or less, from dialing to "hello." The phone company made it all possible by using their equipment to hook up your special pair of wires to the wires of your friend in Tokyo.

Ma Bell used to collect charges from phone to phone. From now on, unless I permit the phone company otherwise, their concern will stop dead at a tiny terminal box on an inside or outside wall of my home. From that point inward, the phone and wiring will be mine to worry about. A few of the new companies have been getting away with charging a monthly "rental" fee for wiring installed in homes in years gone by. In this author's opinion, consumer groups should demand removal of such wire rentals. Failing that, invite the phone company to come in and haul out all their crummy telephone lines. But if so much as one chip of paint is defaced, they will have to be prepared to repaint your home.

Everything that I used in the house—the main phone, the extensions, cables, plugs, bells, chimes, whistles, answering machines, dialers, amplifiers, conference callers, even gadgets to turn my lights on and off by phone—all of them can be mine.

It is perfectly legal for me to buy my own telephones and accessories and hook them into my own home or small business telehone system, as long as they don't do anything nasty when I hook them up to the terminal box, and thus make them part of the local, national, and international network.

If I steal equipment and am caught, I can be sent to jail.

If I find it lying around, I should make reasonable efforts to make sure it's in good shape before using it.

If I buy it at a phone store, swap meet, garage sale, or auction, I'm going to be responsible for installing it and keeping it

24

in good working order or have somebody else do the work for me. And I'll be paying my money for it.

Although it is entirely possible to "hard wire" any residential system by simply twisting wires together and taping them, it's a shortsighted economy. During the first two years of divestiture, competition lowered the cost of new wire, good modular plugs, and sockets to the point where virtually any do-it-yourselfer can install a system every bit as well as most professionals. The only tools you need to do most jobs are a screwdriver and a pair of scissors. Maybe some electrical tape. That's it. Enthusiasts can add pliers. Super-technicians may want to get into soldering irons, meters, and all kinds of thingamabobs. That's okay. Not long ago, I completely "re-phoned" a relative's house. I replaced the original handset, added three extension telephones, and did the whole job with a screwdriver, pocket knife, hammer, about fifty feet of junk wire, and a fifty-cent box of hardware store staples. It was a lousy job. But it worked.

READY, GET SET, GO!

Your telephone is hooked into the worldwide network of 750 million handsets by two fine wires. That's all. And the wires are capable of conducting only small currents. The AC (alternating current) and DC (direct current) used respectively to ring your bell and carry your conversation are nothing to fear. Obviously, if you're the most delicate of heart in town you should be lying down, not fooling around with do-it-yourself things in the first place!

HERE'S HOW IT WORKS

When your phone is on its hook, the weight of the receiver pushes down on a double-function switch in its innards. When somebody dials your number, the signal shoots into your local central office, locates the two wires that are connected to your home phone, and then sends a pulse of alternating current every five seconds to make your phone ring or chime or, in the case of some, light up a bulb. The split second you pick up the receiver, part two of the switch is activated to disconnect the ringing voltage. Your voice connection is then left to carry your message.

Got it? The alternating current is disconnected, the direct current remains.

The two wires that rang your bells then carry your voice, by direct current. The wires are dedicated to your telephone and nobody else's. They connect your home or business to the central office.

No matter the shape or color of your handset, the inner workings of all phones everywhere are about the same. The plastic cord emerging from your present phone base may contain two, four, six, or even fifty wires. The important thing is that only two of these "conductors" are needed to ring another phone and provide the communications path for your conversation.

Although you and I might have no need for more than two conductor wires for all of our residence telephones, it is a good idea to string a phone line with additional pairs of wires when we begin working on our homes. The extra conductors can be used later on for buzzers, lights, bells, even extra phone lines—or "trunks," as they are called—between your home and the central office. A trunk is nothing more than a pair of wires identified by a unique phone number at the central office.

Believe it or not, this one pair of wires can hook up not only our telephones but an assortment of other modern gadgets that connect us to the whole world. In fact, now that most of our long-distance telephone calls are sent by microwaves and bounced off satellites 22,300 miles out in space, it is accurate to say that the two tiny wires into our homes connect us with not only the world, but the entire galaxy!

WIRES AND CABLES AND THE MODULAR JACK

Unlike the stranded, heavy wires used to operate your vacuum cleaner, the phone lines are usually made of light, single-strand conductors, each in its own separate-color covering and all within a colored plastic coating, most often beige. There'll usually be four, six, or eight conductors within each outer covering. Look at the sets in figure 6. Both items in figure 6 are examples of four single conductors within one sheath. At left are plain-ended wires—inside red, green, yellow, and black insulation. They can be twisted clockwise under the screws and held in place. At right are the same type wires, 22-gauge copper, fitted with spade connections that can be fastened under screws or bent over, flattened, to slide into modular connectors.

Sometimes the wires within the sheath at right will all be the same color insulation but the spade connectors at the ends will be color-coded. And usually the important ones will be the red in combination with the green or yellow. Consider the fourth wire as a spare. And usually the green and yellow will both be retained under the same screw or in the same slot of the all-important *modular jack*. Figure 7 illustrates the single most important device in the system.

There are millions upon millions of these tiny gizmos in use today fastening the base cords of telephones to baseboard sockets. They can be snapped into and out of sockets and moved from place to place. There are several varieties of them in use. Their sole purpose is to connect the two wires (sometimes three) from the phone base to the two wires in the socket.

In figure 6 we saw raw wire ends—called "pigtails"—which, if you desire, you can simply hook up directly to telephone base cords. Strip back an inch of insulation, twist together the wires you plan to connect, and tape them up with electrical tape or sticky paper. And good luck!

A step-by-step procedure for installing this type of connection system appears as Appendix A, beginning on page 161.

A HARD LOOK AT INDOOR WIRING

Every wiring job is going to be different. Some modern apartments and homes come complete with all wiring for telephones concealed within the walls, usually ending in junction boxes on the opposite sides of the room from where you want them.

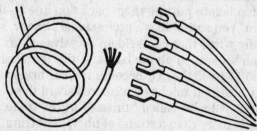

6 / PIGTAILS AND SPADES A PRIMER ON WIRING

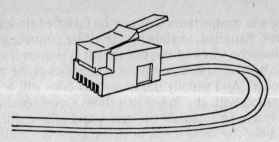

7 / MODULAR JACK A CLOSE-UP OF A GREAT INVENTION

Old houses will probably have old wiring tacked around the baseboards. No matter how old it is, it'll probably work well if all wire endings are scraped clean of corrosion. Old terminal sockets are always reusable as junctions as well as clip-on points for modular sockets.

Older apartments are usually interlaced with ancient, old, new, and futuristic wiring trailed in and out by generations of phone company installers. The locations of the original entry terminals are often shrouded in mystery and cobwebs. Don't let such things worry you.

Your telephone instrument must be fastened somehow to some kind of terminal within your residence. No matter how many coats of paint might be obscuring it, it'll be at the end of your telephone cord. You can open it by undoing a screw or snapping off a cover. You'll see two, three, or four other little screws staring back at you. At least two of them will be holding two incoming phone lines to the wires running into the base of your phone. Loosen those screws and remove the old phone if you plan to replace it. The wires and terminals fastened to the wall will almost certainly be as service-worthy as the day they were installed. Just be sure to sandpaper or scrape them clean of corrosion before putting them back "on line"—that's a technical term. You sound like a professional already, see!

The only wires that can seldom be salvaged are the flexible wires from sockets to phone bases. If the terminals have been ripped loose, or if they've become frayed, bruised, nicked, or just plain scruffy it might be wise to discard them. They're not really wires. They're called "tinsels" in the trade. Essentially, they're little more than a strand of fiber, like string, dusted with metallic material, for electrical conduction. You might repair torn ends by crimping on new spade connectors. Sometimes you can use ultrafine, uninsulated wire to bind a tiny hook of heavier wire in place. Try to tin-solder the assembly, lifting the iron before the fiber is scorched. Such repairs are typical of frustrations that can be encountered in wiring without approved connectors. (See Appendix A.)

No matter what kind of point-to-point cabling you use, however, strive to make it mechanically strong as well as electrically dependable. If you're using salvaged wire, check it as you go for shorts and opens. Start out with two good rules in mind:

☎ Use the already-installed wiring put in place by professionals as much as you can.

☎ Branch out in all the directions you desire using modern, fresh wiring designed for telephone use, most likely 22- or 24-gauge, preferably with not fewer than four conductors within the outer sheathing. It can cost from 2 cents to 5 cents a foot at your electronics, department, or hardware-variety store, but it'll be worth it. Most supermarkets are starting to carry it in 50-foot rolls, priced about $2.50. Try to find four-conductor wire, at a minimum.

Tack it into place with insulated staples knocked home gently with artistic taps of a hammer. If you want it to look truly professional, buy a staple gun, such as the Arrow model T25, with quarter-inch rounded staples, about $17. Conceal the wiring as best you can. If you sneak the cabling under carpeting, okay, but fish it under the padding under the carpet if you can or at least scratch out a little trough for the cabling to rest in peace, preferably off the heavy-traffic lanes in the house.

And again, when you reach the point of termination, think modular, huh? And go for it. A $3 modular socket screwed neatly above a baseboard will not only look better but it'll be handy for connecting and disconnecting phones and other accessories. It'll certainly be more dependable than a clumpy, lumpy black-taped clod of wiring, which we were trying to discourage you from using.

BACK TO THE JACK

The modular jack fits into the modular socket, which often is incorporated into a fitting called a modular plate.

Figure 8 demonstrates such a terminal. It can be fitted over a standard metal box set into the wall or it can simply be held in place by two screws, the socket dropped back behind the wall surface, fastened to the two phone wires.

Another modular socket style is illustrated in figure 9. This one mounts on the surface of a wall or baseboard, again, held in place by two ordinary screws, the wires fastened behind.

An interesting combination of terminals is pictured in figure 10. It has the standard modular opening on the side, a four-prong connector on the face. You'll encounter plenty of screw-type terminals and four-prong terminals, such as the one shown in figure 11, if you're doing a new installation in an older house or apartment. If they are in locations that are satisfactory to you, don't move them. Most department stores and all electronics shops have a variety of adapters that'll enable you to convert older terminals to the modern *modular connector*. They'll range from $1.50 to $5 each. The important thing is they'll provide you decades of quality service.

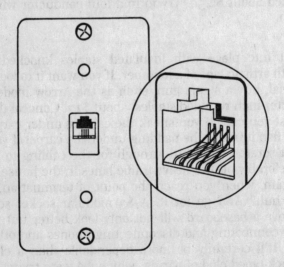

8 / MODULAR SOCKET CLOSE-UP OF THE OTHER HALF

When you begin thinking about installing a homemade telephone system one of your most productive moves will be a trip through your local phone market or department store's telephone displays. You'll be amazed at the number of adapters available (some samples on page 121). You can of course do the job without spending money on adapters, by twisting the wires together and covering the bare connections with almost any kind of sticky tape, but it won't look attractive and it might prove undependable. Loose, fragile connections may cause static, create disconnects, pop out busy signals, and cause other problems for you and your local phone company.

Under the new rules of the game, if the company repairperson has to come out to unscramble your eggs there'll be a dazzling charge for repairs on your next bill. Bear in mind that a few dollars spent now for quality work will be a one-time charge, well worth it in most cases. As you'll read when you discover my pal Charlie, you can save hundreds of dollars using the new modular terminals. Go drape, scrape, and tape if you desire. But the new and nifty little sockets and connectors, with real telephone wires, might be a better way, even if you have to start with only one position in the beginning. Go carefully. Go thoughtfully. Go modular.

TERMINALS

The wiring and terminal devices we've been discussing have been designed in anticipation of a new approach to telephone technology. Ma was looking to reduce her labor and equipment costs. We will get the benefits of her planning. Let's review!

Your local phone company brought the wiring to your present residence in years past. Under the old rules, they then installed all the wiring and the equipment which they had made in their own factories and sent you monthly bills for renting the equipment and the access to the vast network of their lines.

Today, things are different.

The local phone company will terminate the wires from their central office in a plastic or metal box like the one pictured in figure 12. The terminal in figure 12 will accommodate one incoming trunk line—one pair of wires. Get the idea?

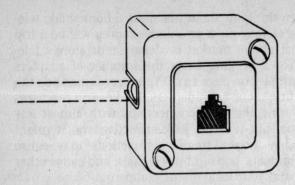

9 / MODULAR SURFACE MOUNT A STAND-OFF TERMINAL

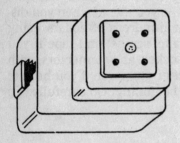

10 / MODULAR WITH ALTERNATIVES FOR DIFFERENT TERMINALS

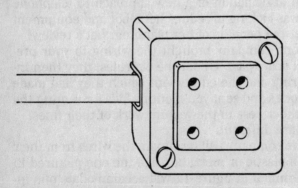

11 / FOUR-PRONG MILLIONS STILL IN USE WORLDWIDE

32

The phone company will place the terminal as close as practical to the point you request, somewhere on an inside or outer wall of your residence. The central post will be attached by a heavy wire to the nearest secure ground, such as a cold water pipe. The two outer connectors will be your connections to the great big world. And just in passing, these connections are really fuses. In the event the outside lines are struck by lightning or thwacked by a falling high-voltage line the fuses will go "pfffsssttt" and any electrical charge will be diverted from your phone system to the ground. The terminal box, no matter what your local phone company might call it, such as SNI (Standard Network Interface) or NI (Network Interface) or DPA (Demarcation Point Arrangement), is essentially the point where the phone company ends its line from the central office and where you can begin your internal home wiring. Your local company should pay for it, but you may have to argue with them about it.

A word of warning about your local company. They learned their lessons at Ma Bell's knee, and that old girl can be foxy. Your local company may, for example, try to wheedle you out of a few extra dollars when you return your rented telephone to their office and say, "I'm using my own equipment now, thank

12 / TERMINAL UNIT WHERE MA BELL ENDS AND YOU BEGIN

you. Here's your old phone back. Just stop charging me rental for it, okay?!"

The local company's employee might wheeze a bit and mutter something about a $5 or $10 switch-over charge. Don't let the phone company get away with it. First ask politely and if need be wind up screaming for the manager. All you are obliged to do, in some locations, is provide the FCC registration number of your new telephone.

Similarly, your local company will try to extract one-time or monthly charges for the connection box. Again—fight back. Some phone companies and phone stores will not only give you the box free of charge, they'll hand you a free conversion kit to make sure you get a good socket for your main telephone.

If confronted by a surly employee, grasp your handset firmly in your fist, about chest high. Squint slightly, give a little Humphrey Bogart lip twitch, and say, "Listen pal, some phone outfits, including New York, pay customers five bucks for returning their telephones, see?" You thus reach out and touch your local company where it lives, in the pocketbook. After all, the folks in the back room will polish up your relic and sell it all over again at a profit, to somebody, somewhere, sometime. Remember, AT&T's income for twelve months ending August 31, 1982, was $11,859,000,000. That's $68,628 every three minutes round the clock. She's not hurting, and her offspring, the Seven Sisters, are asking the public utilities commissioners for huge increases in revenue, for the most part getting them.

If ever in doubt, assume that they are out to beat you for a dime, preferably a quarter. In the new competitive world they'll have to be watched even closer than usual. For example, if you just accept your telephone bills each month as gospel, without checking for errors, charges for calls not made, you'll have only yourself to blame. Recently, in my own personal bill there were two long-distance calls charged, neither of which had been made from my household. We received credit adjustments simply by asking for them.

BACK TO THE TERMINAL BOX

Pictured in figure 13 is a standard multiconnector box typically seen nationwide. This one would accommodate many incoming trunk lines from the nearby central office. From this point the lines would run to various apartments within the building on which it's mounted.

Large office buildings would be loaded with such panels containing thousands of incoming pairs of wires arriving from a central office by way of underground conduits or high overhead poles. No matter their size, shape, or numbers, these are terminal points. They contain screws or bolts and washers that rigidly tie down a wire end.

If the terminal were fitted to accept some kind of snap-in plug we'd refer to it as a socket. The thing that snaps into the socket, in telephone terminology is called a jack or jack plug. Stealing from the electrical trades, the socket is usually referred to as the female and the gadget which snaps into it is the male. Henceforth when we talk about terminals we'll be referring to devices that mark the ending points of wire runs. Sockets will be the devices that jacks and plugs can readily be snapped in and out of.

So, where were we? Let's start at the main terminal, the point where the wires from the phone company's central office arrived at your residence or business. Now you can begin using or restringing the wires already in your location or adding on new cable runs. Maybe the existing wiring in your location will be suitable. It's yours. The phone company has a yearning to get in there and take it back but you know and they know it would not be cost-effective or practical.

☎ SUMMARY

Let's review and double-check our progress. The phone company took our order for a terminal box and assigned a phone number (let's say it is 555-4699 in area code 213). They dropped the line to the terminal and you started running three-pair cable (six wires in one covering) from the terminal through the kitchen, under the cabinets to a modular terminal in the hallway. The important thing to remember about modular connectors is that the wires to or from the main phone are always fastened to the *two center positions* of any jack or socket. Look at the extreme close-up of this one in figure 14. It's a six-slot connector but only four connectors are installed in it.

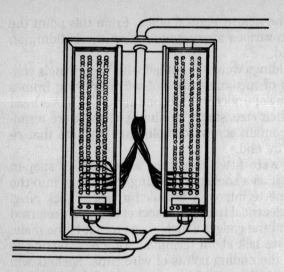

13 / MULTILINE TERMINAL THEY'LL ALWAYS BE WITH US

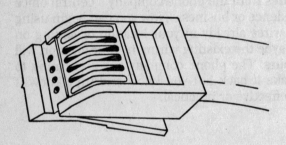

14 / EXTREME CLOSE-UP OF MODULAR GET TO KNOW ONE

We'll still use the two center terminals. The same requirement holds true for the socket. Trace the visible connectors and fasten the two wires to the lugs leading to the center pair of connectors. And usually that'll be with wires that are red and green in color, between phone base and terminal socket. If the cable is plastic-covered the inner wires may be plastic-covered too, usually with blue, orange, green, brown, slate, and white coverings. We're ready to hook up our phones!

2 INSTALLING YOUR FIRST MAIN TELEPHONE

There's a dandy little switch inside every standard rotary dial telephone. Between "rest stops" its purpose is to click the circuit open and closed according to the number a person has dialed. The pulses click at a rate of ten switches per second. The rotary dialer eliminated central office operators, who asked, "Number, please?"

The rotary-dial telephone was just one of hundreds of astonishing achievements by AT&T's Bell Laboratories, innovative devices that helped create the world's largest communications company. Rotary dialers seemed indestructible. They stood unchallenged for efficiency and durability through a half century. The only things able to stop them appeared to be sledgehammers and explosives.

Nevertheless, high-anxiety people in high-speed circumstances were frustrated by the dreary business of waiting for the dial to return to its rest position before the next digit could be dialed.

In the sixties, again prompted by Bell Labs, the Touch-Tone® system of pushbutton communications was introduced. The modern pushbutton telephone was different from anything ever attempted before. It operated on spectacular new concepts. The differences between rotary and pushbutton might be compared to the differences between mule cart and spaceship. The fastest rotary system can open and close switches mechanically in tenths of seconds. The pushbutton instruments theoretically operate in one-billionth parts of a second, electronically. The rotary is noisy, mechanical. The pushbutton generates tones.

Let's take an example that'll help you understand the push-button telephone device and the extraordinary telephone system that we are pledged to protect even while we're playing amateur installers with it in our homes and offices.

FROM MECHANICAL TO ELECTRONIC

The rotary-dial telephone, as described, is a mechanical switch operating in much the same manner as your light switch. You click the button to turn the "juice" off and on. The clicking in your rotary phone is dramatically faster than you could do by hand. It turns the current off and on to another switch at your central office, which moves from position to position with each digit dialed.

If you'd like to sound like an old pro in telephony, you'd call the phone a Type 80 Wheel (500 series) and the switching process at central office the "leap and lurch" or "jump and jerk" system of making connection with your target. The switches do, in fact, run up and down, in and out on shafts as commanded by the successive "offs" and "ons" of your dialing, "1," "2," "3," up to "0" (which is labeled "operator"). The noise inside a mechanical switching office at the phone company is deafening.

15 / BASIC INSTRUMENTS ONE ROTARY, ONE PUSHBUTTON

TURNING OFF THE NOISE, SPEEDING UP THE SYSTEM

When Ma Bell's Lab geniuses came up with "Touch-Tone" ®
the clicks became beeps. When you pushed the "1" button a
very special combination of two audible frequencies was gen-
erated within the instrument—one fairly high, one fairly low,
both in the range you could hear. You could imitate the sounds.
Squeak out a low "beep" and a high "beep" and try to imagine
what they'd sound like if they acted together. Each number as
well as two extra buttons produces a different combination of
tones, standardized all over the world. If you simply must know
the technical details of it all, here they are.

It's called Dual-Tone Multifrequency Dialing, DTMF!

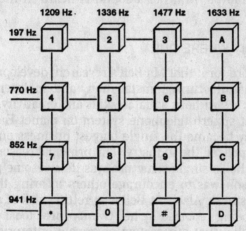

16 / DTMF HOW CLICKS WERE REPLACED BY BEEPS

When you press the digit "1" on your dial pad, the tiny oscillator within your telephone set "beeps" one tone from the
"high numbers" across the top (in this case 1209 Hz) and
merges it with another of the tones from the "low numbers"
seen here in the vertical column (in this case 197 Hz). Each
digit on the phone merges a different set of hertz numbers, the
word *hertz* meaning "cycles."

2 is a combination of 1336 Hz and 197 Hz.

The digit 9 combines 1477 Hz and 852 Hz—got it?

The * and # symbols will be used increasingly for banking
and other signaling codes into computers. The 1633 Hz avail-

ability is used on special dials with 16 "pushbuttons" in sophisticated applications, as illustrated in figure 16. So when you pushbutton a number, you're squirting pairs of tones from your phone, out along the two wires connected to your nearest phone company switch building.

At that central office, the beeps coming from your house enter electronic switches that have no "speakers" and thus are silent. It's a spooky feeling to stand inside a bank of modern switches and know they are usually in control of 50,000 telephones, those in use going "beep beep beep," chasing their targets up the street, across the country, or around the world, noiselessly, making the two-wire connection that enables Willie to talk to Mildred. And not a sound is heard in the switching room.

GIVE CREDIT WHERE DUE

Take my word for it that Ma Bell's research, development, engineering, manufacturing, installation, and maintenance men and women are without equal in skills and creativity. They gave us the most superb telephone system on planet Earth. In the process they became the single biggest business on the globe. They monopolized the industry. The principal reason for breaking up Ma Bell's single structure was its awesome power. The second reason was to encourage others to bring their talents into the business. Also, Ma Bell was getting sick of subsidizing the losses being reported by her twenty-three local companies. It's reasonable that our system of private enterprise could be threatened if only one player was allowed in the game.

That's the nuts and bolts of it. No magic. As Nikola Tesla, the truly disciplined inventor, knew from the beginning and as Alexander Graham Bell learned by trial and error, it was a matter of fastening the right wire to the right coil or other component and applying a shot of electrical energy to the right place—in Bell's case, a spill of battery acid, by accident. Everything since that time has been only an improvement on that original design. I refer to Tesla because he attacked problems systematically, the way Bell Labs do today. You might be surprised to hear there are phones already being tested that "press your buttons" after you call out a special code word, then start repeating the numbers you want "dialed." Coming soon to your nearby phone retailer. Obviously the spoken "code word" brings you security as well as convenience, assuming nobody hears you call it out. So they're working a way of dialing or touching it out. It prevents strangers from running up huge bills on your phones.

For the time being, pushbutton phones that operate on tones are the state of the art. So is the modular connector. The new long-distance services such as Allnet, Sprint, MCI, and ITT Longer Lines are now dependent on tone phones, although they've been advised to make them work on rotary dialers, pronto.

Nevertheless, pushbuttons are more attractive and work so much faster, they're the big deal nowadays. They'll make the added gadgets and gizmos easier to add into your circuitry. And during the first two years of divestiture, I've reached the conclusion that for 95 percent of people it's a lot smarter to buy your own equipment, install it yourself, and stop renting any telephone equipment.

NEW TELEPHONES

The economics of Ma Bell's telephones can best be understood by examining the system, until recently the *only* system.

My own rotary dialer came with the service I ordered installed in my residence eight years ago. My monthly subscriber service—that is, the dial tone—was then regulated at $4.75, but I was billed $6.50. Freely translated, that meant I was paying $1.75 a month to rent the instrument from the phone company. Service charges for a color telephone, which doesn't cost the phone company anything extra, are even higher in some areas. During its ninety-six months of service I paid $168 for my instrument, which in fact had cost my regional Bell Telephone company a paper charge of $6.00 to purchase from its manufacturer, another AT&T subsidiary called Western Electric. Not a bad return on capital investment, eh?

Eight years ago there was no way I could have bought that telephone without immense negotiations, paperwork, and legalities.

Locally, today, it'll cost me $2 per month to rent a comparable phone from the phone company, and the monthly charge for the basic service will almost certainly be doubled by the time this book is in print. It will almost certainly *triple* as soon as the company thinks the time is right for such a move.

Let's see what's available on an outright purchase basis. The telephone companies in many areas may now invite you to buy the equipment you are renting that is already installed in your home. Unless it's less than say, ten years old, and is sturdy and reliable, it'll often be cheaper to buy new equipment at a phone store. Do comparison shopping, okay?

Our familiar and reliable old friend the rotary dialer, also referred to as the "500 series," comes in all colors, complete with coiled cord, seven-foot cord, and modular plug. Pushbutton phones like the basic model pictured here are replacing the rotary dialers. They're beginning to flood the market, made in Japan, China, and Haiti. Most come with a modular plug. Look for sturdy construction.

There are dozens of versions of the style shown in figure 17, often called "French Decorator." Do you want the white with gold trim? Or more filigree? Cheapie?—$30. The "top of the line" in plastic—$100. In real gold trim—$200.

This modernistic look in figure 18 is called "Slim" or "Pulse," depending on the retailer. Several versions of this style feature an automatic redialer, which redials the last number you called at the push of one button. Cheapies sell for as little as $4.95. Forget 'em.

Does figure 19 look different? It is. No cord between handset and base. You can stroll through the room while using it! The cheaper versions start at $70. The 1,000-foot walkaways start at $100. But quality will cost you double those amounts.

The two-in-one model illustrated in figure 20 works best with cord. It'll automatically dial up to sixteen numbers. The long-cord model starts at $90. The wireless style will cost $250!

Since 1977 it's been legal to own and connect your own telephone, but few people knew it. And AT&T didn't rush to tell you. Regional phone companies at one time insisted on seeing each instrument and certifying it for service even though you'd bought and paid for it. Not anymore.

17 / INSTRUMENT DECORATOR MODEL

You'll have to check with your local phone company to get some reasonable notion of what you are paying to rent their instruments. Some styles, such as the Princess®, add $4 a month to your bills. In some areas, fancy handsets rent for $10 monthly. That's $48 to $120 per year extra for the style. You can buy comparable units for that amount or less.

18 / INSTRUMENT PULSE, TRIMLINE OR SLIM

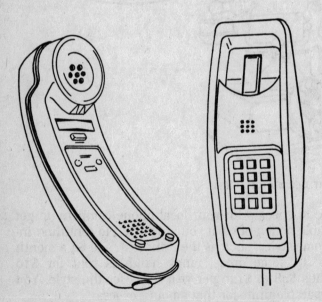

19 / INSTRUMENT CORDLESS, PUSHBUTTON, WIRELESS

20 / INSTRUMENT CORDLESS PUSHBUTTON WITH AUTO-DIALER

Just remember—if you buy your own equipment and it breaks down, it's your problem. You may feel somewhat broken down yourself after paying service charges if you ask the phone company to come out and repair it. In most cases it'll be a lot cheaper to junk the faulty equipment and replace it with alternate instruments. You'll read more about simple troubleshooting in chapter 9.

SECONDHAND MERCHANDISE

Not long ago I bought six bright and shiny telephone sets for $10, total. The modular lines and plugs alone were worth the price. If and when any of my household phones don't function, I'll replace the mugwump with another one and cannibalize the failed instrument. The good pieces are worth salvaging.

If you haven't got a couple of instruments cluttering up your storage closets already, you won't need to travel far to find some. They're popping up by the millions at swap meets and in garage sales, secondhand stores, and thrift shops nationwide.

Will the phone company attempt to scour them out of the market? It's impossible. It is certainly not cost-efficient to chase down one illegal telephone sale. Cost/profit has now become the name of the game, remember? I for one would applaud the efforts of phone companies that diligently go out after telephone thieves who deal in huge numbers of sets.

When I used to go phone shopping, I'd turn the sets over and examine the base plates. First of all, I preferred metal-based telephones. And the physical condition of the rubber feet on phone sets would tell me plenty about how they'd been used or abused. Most often I was looking for a "property of" label or die imprint. I neither needed nor wanted to buy stolen property. And yet I know of no case where any individual has been tracked down and prosecuted for such one-item thievery. That entire question is one you'll have to examine for yourself. Make your own decision.

Another thing. Theoretically, you're required to advise the phone company if and when you are going to install your own equipment. Most store-bought telephones will carry a label on their base noting two numbers, the first an FCC register and the second a ringer equivalency code. Ringer equivalency should be close to 1.0. It's a technical measurement of how much electricity it will require to ring the bell, technically called impedance. The phone company may want to know your FCC number and it will expedite your billing changeover if you call them with it. If they insist you bring the instruments in for inspection, you can tell them to forget it.

Unless an individual is caught red-handed swiping a telephone, it's very unlikely any police system or phone company would dare make a fuss about anyone having a telephone set whose base bears the imprint "Property of Such-and-Such Telephone Company."

It won't always be this way. Already, the telephone companies are looking for techniques to "secure" their equipment more satisfactorily. For the foreseeable future, however, it'll be next to impossible to threaten any individual who is simply trying to get good telephone service at the best price.

Don't feel distressed about AT&T, the Bell Telephone system, its management, or its union personnel. They've all had the field totally to themselves, in happy monopoly for decades.

CEILING
MOLDING

STAPLE TO
BASEBOARD

WIRE
UNDER
RUG

BASEBOARD
MOLDING

21 / WIRING DIAGRAM SOME HOW-TO'S ON CABLING

Even the official publication of the Communications Workers of America (AFL-CIO) states repeatedly, month after month, that the breakup of Ma Bell's grip on the communications industry will ultimately end up as a benefit for Big Business, their Big Union, and even you, the long-neglected consumer!

So there you stand in your old or older or ancient home or apartment. You know you're about to take that big step of getting rid of that grubby old instrument with the ratty, twisted-up cords. You trace the wire from the base of the phone down to some kind of terminal, usually seven, twelve, or twenty-five feet away (the normal lengths of telephone cords). Happy days! You've got a modular connector. You squeeze the tiny lug on the jack and the terminal snaps out of its socket.

Ah, no. You find a scrungy, painted-over, ugly little lump of a box. You mess with it, removing a screw or unsnapping the cover until you reveal the connecting wires. Go to your phone store and buy some kind of adapter that'll suit your wishes and, also, match up snugly with the connector on the new or used phone you've acquired. You make sure the new unit is working by testing it in someone else's socket. Or you use the battery test described in Part Three.

Now what? You start saving money by disconnecting the old, rented phone. If you just can't wait to unscrew the connections, snip the cord with scissors and rush the instrument back to your local telephone company store. So what if somebody calls you while you're gone? You're not there to answer it anyway.

MAKING IT WORK

The receiver or handset of the telephone is connected to the base, most often by a plastic-sheathed cord which returns to its coiled position when the user hangs up. The truly interesting thing most people don't realize about their receiver is that an exotic piece of equipment feeds just the right amount of the user's voice into the earpiece, no matter how loudly or softly the talker speaks into the mouthpiece, also called the transmitter.

The wire dangling at the base of the telephone is the important one for the amateur installer. How's it look? Think it's hooked up right? It should rarely be necessary for the amateur to open the base to start looking around. If the phone doesn't operate at once when it's plugged in, you can skim through the trouble shooting section in Part Three. If you don't find an easy answer there, you can be sure it is a tricky problem. You'll want to haul your phone unit to a repair shop for an estimate or toss it away and get another.

The wire connection from phone base to terminal is the key to most phone problems. The plastic-sheathed cable may match the color of the instrument, in which case you can be sure the wires within it will be covered with plastic insulation in assorted colors. If the plastic cable is colored silver, it might contain several wires that are not color-coded—don't let it worry you.

If there is not a modular plug on the end of the cord already, you might want to consider buying a modular-equipped cable before fussing with it any more.

If the wires aren't color-coded, if the wire ends in the "spade" connectors pictured back in figure 6, you'll see that the connectors are coded by colored paint. Usually, there'll be three wires, sometimes four, occasionally five. The red and green wires should be the important ones. Next in importance is the yellow (which will probably work best if fastened under the green wire terminal). In most hook-ups, the phone won't ring unless the yellow wire is fastened under the same terminal as the green.

Either the black wire or the white wire within the cable (or both of them) will probably be inactive. Unless you decide to use them later for other purposes, you'll be able to ignore them forever. On rare occasion, a red or yellow or green connector will come apart, probably near the connector device or plug. Open the phone base and replace the clunky wire with one of the black or white "spares."

If you're in doubt about the integrity of the wire, if it's bruised-looking, frayed, or patched, do yourself a favor and get rid of it. Replace it. The whole thing!

If you have a phone shop nearby, the salesman there will be pleased to sell you a new and serviceable cord and probably show you how to install it if you take the telephone instrument right into the store with you. Department store personnel may not be so knowledgeable. You won't get answers if you don't ask questions.

Most phone cords are seven feet long. If you like more movement, try a twelve-footer. It'll cost you approximately $4, complete with modular attachment. Some stores will sell you a twenty-five-foot cord for $5 or $6. Another add-on, which you'll find in the upcoming chapter on gadgets and gizmos, is an *extension* for your existing modular phone cord.

THE EXCEPTIONS TO THE RULES

At most one time in ten, you'll encounter a phone set with more than four or five connectors emerging from the sheath. On rare occasions the red and the green will not produce the desired sound when you touch them across the incoming telephone lines. Just keep switching the combinations until you do get a pair that provides your phone with a dial tone. Then keep probing until you find the wire that makes the thing ring! This process may require the cooperation of a friend who will phone your number until the wires are correctly positioned. Again, remember—usually, the *red* wire will be fastened to one of the incoming wires and the *green* plus the *yellow* will be fastened to the other incoming wire. It'll depend on how the inner parts of the set are wired.

There are in existence a few hundred thousand unique, specialized Westinghouse instruments. The pushbutton pads on certain Westinghouse phones were wired in such a way that the phone simply wouldn't function for voice or ring unless wired into the incoming wires with correct "polarity." It's unlikely that you'll stumble across any. Most of them have already been recalled and re-wired for routine connections.

If two or three different telephones all fail to respond to your ministrations and pokings, you can be sure there's a break somewhere between the first terminal box (where the phone company ended its work) and your first telephone terminal block (where you concluded your inside wiring for the main phone).

You can't get hurt by probing around with the ends of the wires, unless you have health frailties whereby the occasional "tingle" might trigger an adverse reaction. If you feel insecure, wear rubber gloves if you don't believe me. Or grasp the ends of the wires with a bundle of potholders held in your hand. The amount of current available even to the ringing circuit is min-uscule.

If you'd like to double-check your telephone instrument, glance ahead to the battery test in the trouble shooting section (page 123), Part Three. It's the easiest and cheapest way to know positively whether you have a good or faulty instrument.

Again—remember—the modular connectors are almost al-ways set up to function using the two wires in the center of the plug or socket. A second incoming trunk can be fastened to the next outermost connections.

Modular plugs and sockets are set up to accommodate six connectors. Occasionally, the connectors will be left out of the outer slots. There may only be four copper-bright contacts star-ing back at you when you peer at the connection points. Work with the pair in the center!

☎ SUMMARY

When installing telephone instruments you anticipate de-pendable service. Frequently, older, long-used handsets will prove to be more rugged than recent models built for a competi-tive price. A few years ago the accent was on building things to last, not to fail when the warranty expired.

Think over your priorities when setting out to buy new or used telephones.

Price? Obviously, old rotaries are cheapest. Don't be hesitant about unscrewing the earphone cover and mouthpiece. The units inside may drop out in your hand, because they were made to sit on connector rings while the caps were screwed on. Some are screw-connected.

You can disinfect the outside of most used telephones with-out fear of hurting them. Use any standard disinfectant with a moist cloth and scrub away at the mouthpiece and earphone. The plastic surfaces will shine well after vigorous application of soap and moist toweling. If you wish to scour out scratches, get a plastic polish from your hardware store.

Color? The colors of telephone sets may be a consideration. Some people even enjoy painting designs on their telephones. There are some paints that take well to the highly polished plastic. But the parts inside all of them are basically the same, as described in Part Four.

Wiring? It's the important item to remember when you go phone shopping. Keep your eyes open for good instruments, but don't forget the cords. And by all means, keep looking for the units that have modular plugs on the wire end.

The items to avoid are those with frayed, ripped-up wires. There's no easy way to install tiny modular jacks on ragged wire ends. Better you skip the whole unit than fool around trying to repair a flawed wire and/or connector.

Again, the reminder! In an initial installation, you can save hundreds of dollars by doing it yourself. If you're moving into a new home or apartment that's been pre-wired for phone service, you can save huge amounts by simply plugging in your own secondhand or new telephones.

The phone company will be delighted to rent you instruments and be responsible for maintaining them. Rule of thumb? If you plan to stay in your location for a year or more, you'll save money by buying your own.

Once your main telephone is in place and working, you'll be hooked. Wait'll you get that first call. A one-second ring followed by a four-second pause. You answer *your* phone, "Hello?" Yikes! You will start searching around for places to hook up more phones. Here's one good example of what can happen to you.

CHARLIE, THE PHONE MAN

My pal, Charlie, is a telephone nut. His home is very conventional, with a kitchen, two bathrooms, two bedrooms, living room, dining area, patio, garage, and a small pool. He has a total of twelve telephones connected. He has two main lines wired to his residence.

One incoming line serves at the main location, the room which ordinarily is used as his "home office."

An extension is beside his bed for business calls after hours. It has assorted silencers and answering gadgets attached.

The other ten telephone sets are of various shapes and sizes, most of them pushbutton, half of them still operational in the chiming and ringing department, all operating on the second trunk line to the phone company.

One of the "main phones" is the base unit for his cordless extension. When Charlie goes walking with his dog, he can take telephone calls from as far away as three long blocks in any direction. There are no steel structures or other interferences in his neighborhood.

By dialing his number from any place in the world, he can get his home-built monitor to check his doors and windows, adjust the temperature, turn on the lawn sprinklers, or tell his television to pre-select a favorite program for taping on his videocassette recorder, certain channel, certain time.

There are a dozen other functions he can control by touching the pre-coded buttons on whatever telephone set he happens to be using. He even carries a gadget in his briefcase that can snap over a rotary dialer if he can't locate a pushbutton telephone. The device enables him to run all his home gadgetry by pushbuttons as soon as he has dialed up his number on any standard rotary telephone and snapped his tone generator over the mouthpiece. Another snap-on gadget advises him if his line is being bugged. There's no big mystery about any of it. He installed the entire system by himself, mostly from secondhand parts. The basic Bell company charges for his two telephone lines totaled $14.80 a month before divestiture. Two increases approved by his state's public utilities commission since divestiture have increased the cost to $24.40. The phone company had asked for (but didn't get) increases to $19.50 per line, which would have cost Charlie $39 total. Like the rest of us, he pays extra for his long distance and his toll calls. He uses one of the long-distance services other than Ma Bell and has reduced his long-distance charges 30 percent, enough to offset the increase in base rate. All of these considerations will become evident to you as we proceed through this book. Really, they're very simple, all of them within your capability to do-it-yourself.

3 ADDING EXTENSION PHONES, NO CHARGE

When your main telephone is in place, you can proceed to branch out in all directions within your home or small business, installing extension phones of all shapes, sizes, and usefulness. If you were to have them installed by the telephone company, you'd pay a charge of approximately $50 to $150 to have a modular outlet at each location. Then, if you continued in the "old style," you'd rent the instrument from the phone company at a rate of $2 to $10 per month, per instrument.

The advantage in having your local telephone company do the work and install all the equipment is that they become responsible for its maintenance. If anything fails during service, call them up and a repairperson hustles over to correct all the problems.

There are exceptions to this nifty scheme. Among the seven new so-called local companies, there are changing patterns. They're testing us. Even if we rent their equipment, some will charge for every service call. The charge might be nominal if we are using the equipment we rent from the company. The charge can be beyond belief if the company's repairperson declares it's our own self-owned equipment that is causing problems. We will cover that subject in detail later. We'll show you how to predetermine whether your phone problems are *your* fault or the snafus within the local company and its wires.

WARNING!

In the "new system," it's essential to learn from the business office exactly what *your* charges might be at *your* location (a) if you continue to rent their stuff and (b) if you use your own equipment.

If you have a habit of dropping your telephone into boiling water or watching the dog chew it to bits, you might be well advised to have the phone company do the whole thing. But most of the time, for most of the people, telephone service breaks down outside the residence or office. It's a system failure three out of four times. A system failure is always their problem, not yours.

DO-IT-YOURSELF EXTENSIONS

Assuming you've found or bought extra telephones that would attract you to the idea of adding extensions, the question arises, "How many can I tack on to my system?"

The answer must be vague because it'll depend largely on the distance your residence or business is located from the central office, something you're not too likely to know.

The voltage for the equipment is supplied from the central office. It'll always be constant, at the source, 48 volts in the talking battery. The ringing supply runs from 75 volts to 100 volts of alternating current—not enough to hurt a normally healthy person, however.

The greater the distance from that source to your telephone, the longer the wire that connects you. The wire means resistance in the line. The more telephones in that circuitry, and the longer the wire, the more resistance. That'll reduce the level of electricity reaching you. You might be getting as little as 20 or 25 volts if you're the last person on a line, farthest away from your central office.

You'll only find out by trial and error. In most urban locations, up to five or six *modern* telephones will ring joyfully even though they're being fed from a single line.

Another gimmick you can adopt is to open the phone case and disconnect the wires that are connected to the bell-ringing mechanism. (See Part Four for guidance on internal wiring.) Usually it's easier to lift the yellow wire, leaving the green (called tip) and red (called ring) connected. The voice-carrying circuits will remain intact. You might have ten phones hooked up as extensions, but only three will ring. That's okay, if you can hear the ringers from other locations.

STARTING POINT

You may begin running your wires from the main terminal block where the system enters the house or you can pick up connections at the main telephone socket. Take the most convenient route.

It's important to assert yourself with your telephone company and other utilities. A neighbor of mine, in a condominium with a central "box" for telephone connections bought the first edition of *Kiss Ma Bell Good-bye* and hooked up one extension at the terminal point drop provided by the General Telephone Company, locally.

During the first year, he observed that on a couple of occasions after the local installers had been poking in the box, on other business, they seemed intent on disconnecting his own extension. He would reconnect his lines when the GTE employees departed. After a third disconnect, however, he came to me, raging that the data in the book was wrong or the local company was giving him a hard time. I assured him the book was correct and the company was in error. We simply hung a card on my friend's connection wires at the demarcation drop. "Installer—do NOT tamper with this connection or a complaint will be filed with your supervisor and disciplinary action will be demanded."

For more than a year the connections have been left undisturbed, though we know that several adjustments have been made by the company's workers on other lines in the building.

Let's get back to work.

Even if you only need two wires now, it is always a good idea to install cable with extra conductors, for other purposes and expansion in future years. It really does pay to start out with real telephone cable, say six wires minimum. Salvaged wires might work but won't be as dependable as store-bought cable.

The main idea is to make the wiring as obscure as possible. A handyperson with lots of drills and experience will probably conceal the wiring within walls, behind moldings, and in troughs scratched through the padding under the rug. Most folks settle for something a bit less, such as tacking the wiring as straight and neatly as possible along baseboards, over doorways, behind cabinets and such things.

22 / A MODULAR/FOUR-PRONG PLUG DOUBLE-DUTY DEVICE

Don't try to staple the wire to woodwork, using your desk equipment. An ordinary staple just might pierce the insulation and "short" the conductor within the cable.

Figure 21 suggests some techniques for wiring around interior corners, over doorways, and under window ledges.

Although insulated staples are not the most attractive devices, they're available at low cost in every hardware store. They can be tacked into place readily with a few taps of a light hammer. Or, if you feel like a pro, buy a staple gun designed specifically for fastening phone wires into place. Keep the wiring stretched straight and tight as you move forward, using a staple at least every three feet. When you reach your destination, snip the wires with pliers, knife, or kitchen scissors and hook them up as before.

Shown in figure 22 is an interesting and useful modular/four-prong jack plug that can be fastened easily to a wooden baseboard or even a plasterboard wall. Note how it accommodates either a modular plug or four-prong plug—even both! As before, the two principal phone lines will be attached to the center pair of connectors.

It's good practice to hook up the residential system before connecting the lines at the main terminal. Test each leg of your wiring as you move along.

Although few people are sensitive enough to feel the tingle that sometimes can be felt through the dial tone conductors, the ringing circuit is something else. Almost everyone can feel the electric vibrations if the phone rings just when the installer

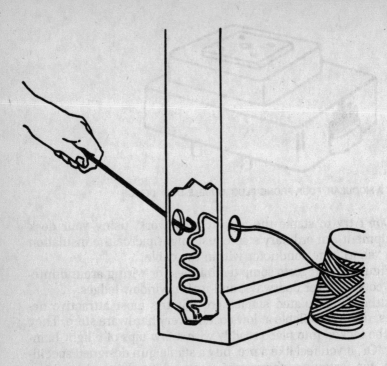

23 / INTERIOR WALL, CROSS SECTION A WAY TO WIRE THINGS

is holding a conductor in each hand. To reduce such unlikely possibilities, wire the system before hooking up to the main terminal box, one wire at a time. Another way to prevent ringing voltage from reaching you while you're adding extensions is to lift the receiver "off hook" at the main telephone.

At the main terminal block or box, simply loosen the fastener, twist one wire around it as before, clockwise, and screw it down. Then proceed to do the same with the second wire. If you feel the least bit wary, simply stand on a dry rug as you do it.

When you plug your extension into the socket, presto—you should hear the dial tone and can make another call to yesterday's friend who soon may be asking you to do the same thing for him or her. You may lose your amateur standing when the word gets around.

That'll be okay, too. It'll be legal. And profitable. And also, ever so much easier the second time around!

58

DO YOURSELF A FAVOR—PLAN AHEAD!

When you begin planning locations for your main telephone and its extensions, map it out on paper, first. Make a bird's-eye view of your premises, as though somebody lifted the roof off your residence or office.

No matter how primitive your drawings of rooms and walls, you'll learn lots of things that'll save you time and money.

☎ You'll discover how the existing phone wiring might be worked readily into your new scheme of things.

☎ You'll see possibilities of shortcuts from room to room. Even if you have to go out and borrow a neighbor's drill to run a couple of holes through partitions, it might be worth it, rather than tacking wires up and over doorways.

☎ You'll more readily determine whether you should connect your extensions one after another, like a string of Christmas tree lights, or perhaps go back to the main terminal to pick up connections for your second, third, and fourth telephones.

There are so many ways to run wires in so many different styles of buildings that you'll be challenged to use your ingenuity.

If there's crawl space under your residence or office, you may wish to run extension lines diagonally under the flooring rather than use extra wires and work hard to make them obscure, going around the perimeter of rooms. If that's a good idea, but you deplore the notion of squirming through such spaces, enlist the help of a friend and his dog or cat, if they're small critters.

Tie a string to the animal's collar and release the little fellow into the crawl space near your terminal box while your neighbor calls his pet from the far side of the building. The animal should make a speedy dash to its owner, trailing the string. Then you can fasten your wire or another heavier cord to the string trailed through by the animal and your connectors will be in place. An extension fishing pole will help thread a wire. Or try tossing a rubber ball with a string on it. Professionals use such devices. Just remember, please don't let your phone wiring lie on damp earth, where, later on, moisture may create problems for your system.

Several years ago, stringing a temporary extension phone for one of my own family members, I trailed a length of antenna wire in and around bushes in the garden. I disconnected the add-on phone a few days later, but I didn't detach the circuit in the terminal box. It was months later, after weeks of intermittent phone static, that I traced the line, now half in and half out of assorted puddles. And at one point the leg of a child's swing was squatting directly over the half-buried wire. No wonder I'd agonized about the back-and-forth, off-and-on nature of the problem. It only occurred when the ground was moist and a child was hauling forward and backward on the metal swing!

I've used a slingshot with a bolt and tie line to launch phone wires through tricky spaces. I've watched a professional use his bow and arrow to sail a wire from point A to point B. I've heard about an installation made by kite flying, dropping the string and kite when it was directly over its destination.

Here's another tip. If I find it helpful to scoot a wire *through* a wall in order to circumvent a long stretch of wire, I rarely go drilling wildly all the way through. As seen in the cross-section view shown in figure 23, I might do better by boring slowly through the best position on one side of a main wall, then stuffing a few feet of string into the small hole. Next, I'll drill a hole, measured off carefully into the wall of the second room, trying to be as close as possible opposite the hole I drilled in the first room.

Then I can begin fishing into the second hole, using a length of coat hanger wire in which I've bent a tiny hook. I can usually pick up a loop of the string hidden within the walls. I pull it through, tie it to my extension cords, and pull the wires neatly into position.

Using this method, I don't need an expensive, super-long drill.

If I encounter a stud or some other obstruction, I've only made a small hole in one wall and I can readily find another spot nearby. If there's any unusual resistance to drilling, I stop, long before I've pierced a hidden pipe or electrical circuit.

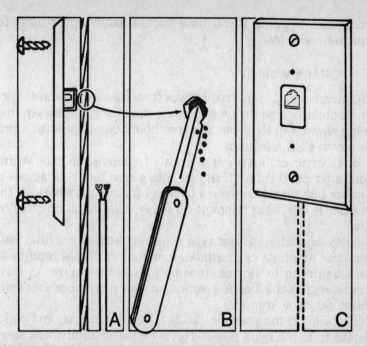

24 / INSTALLING SOCKETS FLUSH AGAINST WALLS

On the general subject of drilling holes in walls, you might remember the following trick for installing modular wall plates. It's not necessary to install a heavy-duty electrical-type box behind the wall in order to add on a modular connector plate. Look at the side view of the connector, as seen in figure 24, part A. The "business" section, as you can see, is just a knobby lump behind the finished plate.

Simply drill a small hole in the wall where you wish to position an extension, then ream it larger with a pocket knife (part B). Most modular plate sockets are less than an inch in diameter. Fasten the two wires to the center pair of connectors, as usual. Shove the wires and plate into position and screw the finished plate to the wall (part C). Plug in your extension and phone your friend!

If you have no space under the floor, you may have some space above the ceiling. Look for an entry to it in a closet or end of a hall. It'll provide another easy way to toss extension wires from point to point, if you have such a dandy opportunity for your new activity.

TEMPORARY WIRING

I've phone-wired more tree houses than I'd care to admit. For a small child or even a teen, there's nothing more classy than being allowed to sleep out in a tree house complete with a real, honest-to-gosh telephone.

But I've never, but never, permitted a phone line to be strung from a terminal through the air into a tree house or across to another building, except on a one-night, temporary basis. If the weather is fair, okay. Hook it up today, remove all of it tomorrow.

Outdoor wiring of that type requires outdoor cabling, with immense amounts of grounding conductors. Trees tend to attract lightning in storms. It simply makes no sense to leave temporary installations in position just because there's an extra phone set lying around.

The same thing goes for garages, barns, cabanas, and patios distant from the main house. Having a party? A business meeting? Got a long job to do in one of the buildings? Okay—string a pair of wires through the air or off the beaten paths and hook up a quickie extension. Just remember to remove the whole system as soon as is practical. Unless it's been installed neatly with the correct indoor/outdoor cabling it can only create problems later on, if not immediately.

☎ SUMMARY

Installing extension telephones here, there, and everywhere through any home or office (assuming the owner doesn't object) is probably easier than installing that all-important, super-neat main telephone.

In fact, some folks who are intent on having lots of extensions but deplore the idea of mind-boggling installation charges will often have the phone company install the main phone, being certain to get a modular jack installation. Maybe a month or so later they can return the phone company's instrument and simply plug in their own unit. It's costly, but may be a practical starting point for the faint-hearted. If you think the phone game isn't becoming deadly, in Los Angeles it'll cost $35 to wire that first phone; in New York $94, if the companies are invited to do it. Then they'll charge you again if they have to come back to fix the mistakes they made the first time. (No, Virginia: There ain't no Santa Claus in the phone business.) In New York particularly, customers seem to take no interest in finding out what's going on, why their charges are so far out of line with the remainder of the world. Don't get me wrong—I love New York. I just don't like anything about their public utilities, any of them. Bah! Humbug! Anyway, let's assume that all-important first terminal is in place. Homeowners can now pick up where the professionals left off. By simply using a double socket or two, they can begin running extensions in all directions from the main phone terminal.

Look at figure 25. It works the same way an everyday three-way plug for electricity functions. It can couple two phones, a phone and amplifier, or phone and answering machine from one outlet. Most stores sell them for approximately $5. Some styles, with wider bars, enable the user to plug one adapter into another, for three, four, or more "outlets."

It's a more expensive way of running extensions, but it'll work for you. In a couple of months, the extra connectors and wiring will have paid for themselves when compared to phone company charges which go on, month after month, year after year!

Personally, I don't like "extension cords" that can get tangled underfoot and generally prove to be a cluttered make-do ar-

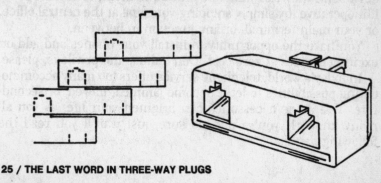

25 / THE LAST WORD IN THREE-WAY PLUGS

rangement. But there are, undoubtedly, situations where the duplex jack plug and socket and a long cord on that extra phone will do a serviceable job for a period of time. One thing for sure, if you don't like it after you've installed it, it's a cinch to snap out of its socket and use it elsewhere.

Again, remember—what you do inside your home with your own homegrown phone system is your own business and nobody else's. It'll require only that you're not sending spurious signals, weird voltages, or super-loud noises out on the telephone line between your premises and the central office.

The phone company will do nothing to discourage you if your installations are reasonably satisfactory. The company will make mumbling sounds about utility regulations. But they regularly improvise themselves. You can have twenty extensions in a five-room house if that makes you happy. It's unlikely that any phone company will be sending you enough signal voltage to ring more than five phones under the best of circumstances. You can try, however. And you can dream up your own schemes. Just don't try to outsmart the phone company. They not only know all the tricks, they invented them. Sooner or later they'll catch up to all the crooks who use gimmick boxes and sophisticated gadgets that purport to beat the company on such things as long-distance charges. And that activity is a genuine felony.

If you do anything to upset the phone service to the other 300 million people in the U.S. and Canada who use telephones in their homes and offices, the phone company has a perfect right, under law, to ask you to stop being a nuisance. If you persist in devilment, they can yank out your equipment, or at least make it inoperative, by simply snipping your line at the central office, or your main terminal, or any junction in between.

You have the opportunity to install your phones and add on exciting devices at zero cost. Don't abuse the privilege, please.

In today's world, telephone service offers too many accommodating possibilities to let it become jammed, flawed, or secondrate. Telephone accessories can brighten your life, as you already know. If you're not too sure, just wait'll you read the following pages.

PART TWO

Telephone Accessories

4 ANSWERING MACHINES

To get a better view of where we're going, let's take another look at where we are. The phone lines which were brought to your location by the phone company terminated in an official box such as we saw in figures 8 and 9. You ran your indoor wiring to telephone locations and hooked up one or more phones, using the two wires, probably red and green (with most likely the yellow fastened to the green), at the phone connection.

If you simply twisted the wires together and/or soldered them and taped them, you have something resembling a clump of spaghetti. Good luck. It may work well, for years to come.

It's to be hoped that you joined the incoming lines to the telephone instrument through a modular connection. Now you can trundle off in all directions. On page 108 you'll discover a display of adapters which will enable you to hook up vast numbers of gadgets to your phone system. Store-bought, they'll all be connectable with the modular types of equipment. If you use duplex connectors you can simply plug in to the extra connection sockets and you'll be in business.

THE ANSWERING MACHINE

Most common of all the accessories that can be added to residence and small business phones is the automatic answering machine. This is the gadget that everybody complains about but nevertheless usually buys on the first flimsy excuse. The price range on new machines tops out at $300 and bottoms at $80, but the very cheap models tend to create more frustrations than they solve.

HOW THEY OPERATE

If you think of answering machines as basically two tape cassette recorders in one box, you'll appreciate their clever characteristics. When you comprehend the answering gadget you'll gain a quick understanding of most telephone accessories.

So, your answering machine is plugged in alongside any telephone, by means of a modular jack and socket (or somehow you've fastened the machine's two wires to the pair that feeds your phone). When the machine feels the tingle of current from an incoming call, it usually waits for a second one, then a third, and springs into action. Without lifting the receiver, a switch triggers into action.

First, the ringing relay is told to "shut up, knock it off," leaving the voice circuit clear through your central office, hither, thither, and yon to the caller's telephone.

Second, the switch starts the motor on tape machine number one, which now begins to play your message, recorded earlier for presentation at this time.

"Hello, this is my answering machine at 555-5555. And I'll be away from this telephone briefly. Please leave your name, phone number, and any brief message and I'll call you back as soon as possible. Wait for the beep signal and then please leave your message."

The machine then goes "beep," which causes another relay switch to wake up and do two things. First, it shuts off the motor on machine number one. Second, it starts the motor on machine number two, which is preset to *record* messages, just like any ordinary tape recorder. It records for a predetermined number of seconds or minutes or until the calling party stops talking, a "pause" which causes everything to cycle back to sleep and wait for the next incoming call.

Easy?

As easy as plugging in a modular jack, if you've provided a socket for it.

This guide for free and easy telephone gadgetry has insisted all along that you should make your own decisions. In answering machines, the best we can do for you is to tell you what's available and what you may wish to look for when shopping for equipment.

There is, in this one area of telephone accessories, one style of answering machine you might do well to ignore, even if you are offered one for free. Any device which requires you to cradle your telephone in such a way that the machine will actually lift the receiver before beginning its operations is almost sure to be very old (by communications standards) and a horror to have serviced by professionals.

Commercial companies that depend on incoming calls for all their business, accepting calls around-the-clock, will invest thousands of dollars to purchase handmade units. In the residential service, however, the $80-to-$300 range provides just about every characteristic most people might require.

There are many reliable brands available, each offering machines at a variety of prices with a range of different features. See the illustrations in figure 26. We'll describe machines and their features related to price. The features noted will give you a checklist of desirable or undesirable characteristics for any price range you select.

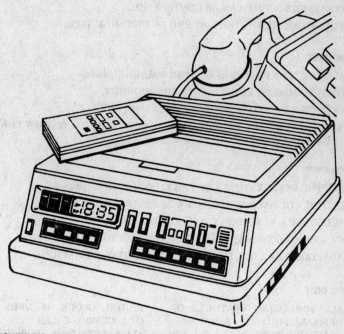

26 / ANSWERING UNIT AN EXPENSIVE MODEL

$80 UNIT

- OFTEN ONE-CASSETTE MACHINES.
- ALL OUTGOING MESSAGES MUST LAST 30 SECONDS.
- MACHINE WILL RECEIVE UP TO 40 INCOMING CALLS, 1½ MINUTES EACH.
- IT'LL HAVE NO COUNTING DEVICE TO LOCATE STARTS AND STOPS.
- MAYBE IT'LL HAVE A FAST-FORWARD TO PASS OVER UNWANTED MESSAGES. MAYBE NOT.
- NO AUTOMATIC SHUT-OFF AT TAPE'S END.

$120 UNIT

- BE CERTAIN THE MACHINE DOES NOT HAVE TO BE RETURNED TO DEALER OR FACTORY FOR CASSETTE AND MESSAGE CHANGES.
- CAPACITY UP TO 120 INCOMING CALLS.
- EASILY CHANGEABLE "IN" AND "OUT" MESSAGE TAPES.
- MONITOR LETS YOU SCREEN INCOMING CALLS.
- TINY LIGHTS INDICATE "ON," "OFF," "RECORDING."
- PLAYBACK VOLUME CAN BE CONTROLLED.
- FULL-CAPACITY SHUT-OFF AT END OF INCOMING TAPE.

$160 UNIT

- ALL THE BEST FEATURES OF $120 MACHINE *plus—*
- HIGHER-QUALITY COMPONENTS THROUGHOUT.
- SELECTOR TO ALLOW OUTGOING MESSAGE ONLY.
- BATTERY-POWERED REMOTE PACK ENABLES YOU TO CONTACT THE UNIT FROM ANY PHONE AND GET ITS MESSAGES.

$200 UNIT

- ALL THE BEST FEATURES OF THE $160 MACHINE *plus—*
- DIGITAL COUNTER FOR NUMBER OF CALLS.
- SELECTABLE RING DELAY, 1–6 RINGS.
- CAN RECORD TWO-WAY CONVERSATIONS AS YOU TALK.
- ADAPTABLE AS A ROUTINE RECORDER, DICTATING MACHINE.

$300 UNIT

- ALL FOREGOING FEATURES OF DESIRABLE QUALITY, *plus—*
- COMPUTER-TYPE INDEX TO LOCATE INCOMING CALLS.
- DIGITAL CLOCK RECORDS TIME OF INCOMING CALLS.
- ALL-ELECTRONIC PUSHBUTTON CONTROLS.

70

- SEVERAL SELECTABLE OUTGOING MESSAGES FOR VARIATIONS.
- VOICE-ACTUATED. SHUTS DOWN WHEN CALLER STOPS TALKING.
- PANEL WILL DISPLAY TIME, DATE, NUMBER OF CALLS, HOW LONG, AND OTHER DATA.
- TELEPHONE BUILT-IN

You pays your money and you takes your choice.

USED EQUIPMENT

Top-of-the-line answering machines can sometimes be found at swap meets. One of the editors of this book commented that she'd located an almost-new version of the $300 device shown above and the seller made an instant "money-back guarantee" deal for $100.

Was it a stolen machine? Probably.

Of course, if you can locate what appears to be a recent model machine with a well-known name, chances are, if it's faulty it'll be serviceable. There's not much that amateurs can do when an answering machine goes blooey. They're among the most complicated of all telephone accessories.

The company that manufactured mine has been out of business for at least five years. I'd never hope to have it factory-repaired. In fact, I once saw a ceiling-high pile of the units being sold "bulk" at $5 each. I would have happily bought a couple to cannibalize—except the seller insisted I purchase a minimum of a hundred of them. No sale!

But does the story give you a picture of how that business functions? It's competitive. Only the very substantial "names" survive.

TROUBLES WITH ANSWERING MACHINES

Used gently, as all electronic equipment should be, answering machines in household use can be trouble-free if used regularly but not nonstop.

1. If there's a crackly message going out from your machine to any caller, your message tape will need replacing. In most machines, it's simply the replacement of a cassette. My own, in normal use, seem to perform excellently for about eighteen months, then deteriorate fast, particularly at the very beginning of the answer tape.

2. The recording heads (and playbacks) in answering machines deserve a bit of swabbing with rubbing alcohol or commercial cleaner about once a year. (They're readily located by removing the cassettes and pressing the "on" button, which on most models will cause the heads to move out into the open.) If you can borrow a demagnetizer, now's the time to use it. If you take your machine to any electronics shop, they'll probably demag your heads for free.

3. If your machine refuses to intercept callers or record their messages, for heaven's sake, double-check your connections before hauling the unit away for repair. Wiggle the wires. Test and retest before hauling your machine to a repair shop. The charges are usually not worth having old machines rejuvenated. If you're bent on repairs, pick repair people who are specialists in the answering machine trade. In many instances the pickup coil will need its contacts cleaned, little more.

LOCATING YOUR PHONE ANSWERING MACHINE

In such a situation, a quick glance reminds the householder that the machine is in the "on" position. So you check it to see if the counting device is different from the last time you looked.

A FINAL PLEA

Some people like to load their greeting messages with jokes, toasts, and stories prior to the beep tone. In my opinion, it's one of the unfunny things that have given the machines a bad reputation. Please keep your outgoing messages short and to the point for the sake of the rest of us.

5 AUTOMATIC DIALERS, REDIALERS, AND AMPLIFIERS

There are good reasons and dumb reasons for adding an automatic dialing system to your telephone service. Good ones first.

Persons with vision problems, for example, may be able to operate rotary or pushbutton phones, but it's certainly a greater convenience to locate one button than to dial seven numbers or more.

Individuals with diseases ranging from arthritis to asthma may find it reassuring to know that a doctor or any other helper can be summoned by simply touching one button on the face of the phone set or its attached accessory panel.

There are two basic styles of auto-dialers. The first is an all-in-one telephone, auto-dialer/redialer, and amplifier. In addition, it has a built-in battery device that'll retain the memory system so that the user can readily unplug the telephone and move it to the extension socket in another room without losing the storage of remembered phone numbers. Don't fuss over those technicalities. Your concern should be whether you want to pay for such options, not how they function.

The most basic instrument will store up to sixteen different telephone numbers, making each seven-digit number available simply by lifting the receiver and touching the one button opposite the name of the individual you'd like to telephone.

The storage of sixteen seven-digit numbers sounds like enough capacity until you begin to think about overseas calls or subscribing to the new long-distance systems that have entered the business. The new systems will require auto-dialers with much larger capacities until "equal access" reaches across the continent.

EQUAL ACCESS

In a nutshell, the words simply mean that the digit "1," which worked splendidly when Ma Bell owned everything telephonic, won't work to connect you into any other system—*yet*. Some different codes will be required at central offices.

When you want to make a long-distance call, the local phone company will be able to send your signal along the system that you have told them you desire to use. When your monthly bill arrives, your long-distance calls will be listed along with the name of the carrier you selected. You will send one check to the local phone company, which in turn will send your long-distance share to the carrier of your choice. Some sellers, such as American Express Company's Express Phone Service®, bill their customers directly, even though their service is bought from the MCI system.

In the meantime, it may be necessary for you to dial numerous digits to connect into any system other than Ma Bell's.

You might want to drop into your local phone shop or an electronics store before you buy. The least expensive and reasonably dependable machine would cost about $50 and could handle thirty different numbers up to fifteen digits each. It would simply plug into a modular jack beside your telephone, using the duplex socket, with an electric plug.

For a bit more money you will at least double the capacity, and the gadget will probably have a built-in digital clock and timer that prudently reminds you of the seconds that are ticking away on your long-distance calls.

They might appear to be intelligent gadgets. Not really. If you have a standard cassette tape recorder and a pushbutton phone, you can demonstrate the whole process for yourself before you buy.

Set the cassette machine running in "record" position, holding the microphone firmly shielded by your fist over the telephone earpiece. And pushbutton an outside phone number. The tones will be recorded on the tape.

Now play them back, this time holding the mouthpiece of the telephone receiver close to the speaker on the cassette tape recorder. If your recorder and its microphone have even a middle-of-the-road quality, the sound just recorded will come beeping out of the tape player into the telephone receiver and—presto—your party should be dialed, just as if you'd done it yourself live instead of on tape!

There you have the whole principle of the automatic dialing machine and the redialer. It's a bunch of numbers on a loop of recorded tape. You have to enter the numbers the first time. From that point forward you'll simply depress the button beside the name you've inscribed on the panel opposite each button. One feather-touch will ring through to your objective.

If the line's busy, some auto-dialers will go on to redial without the touch of another button. Every thirty to sixty seconds it'll ring up the same line, and then sound a tone to get your attention the first time it can make the connection.

CAPACITY OF AUTO-DIALERS

A cheap auto-dialer will store ten to thirty numbers, but the capacity may in fact be only seven digits per number. It'll dial out only local calls of seven digits each! The majority of units handle about sixteen numbers with fifteen digits per number. Expensive machines (in the $100-plus bracket) can usually be found with a capacity to store thirty-two numbers with thirty digits each. It sounds like a great many, but let's take another look. Unless or until your area gets "equal access," you may find yourself dialing or "touching" the following number of digits to complete a call through any of the alternate systems.

	DIGIT COUNT
IT'LL REQUIRE A LOCAL CALL TO THE SERVICE	7
THE SERVICE WILL NEED YOUR ACCOUNT CODE	5
WHEN CONNECTED TO LONG DISTANCE, YOU NEED A SENDER CODE	1
THEN COMES THE AREA CODE	3
AND YOUR FRIEND'S BASIC NUMBER	7
HOW MANY DIGITS DID IT REQUIRE?	23

Overseas calls and institutional systems can add as many as seven more digits to dial!

Limited-capacity auto-dialers usually accommodate longer numbers "per calling point" by simply picking up the extra capacity from other buttons. You can wind up with a so-called sixteen-number machine limited to eight or ten numbers.

You may wish to keep these figures in mind when you go shopping. My own auto-dialer allows me to use one button for accessing the system, then a second button to reach the phone I'm "dialing"—I use a MOOG unit made to sell for $60 that I purchased on sale at the local company's "Phonemart"™ for $24.95 (MOOG's in Buffalo, N.Y.).

AMPLIFIERS

A quality dialer will usually come equipped with a two-way amplifier. Telephone systems carry sufficient power to operate voice circuits for several small earphones and mouthpieces. The tiny voice signal that reaches your instrument can be amplified simply enough by adding on an extra "stage" of power.

Your auto-dialer-with-amplifier will actuate a loud speaker in the unit enabling you to carry on a conversation with your caller even while you wander around the room, going about your routine chores while you talk.

The same amplifier will enable several people in the room to hear your caller and talk back, even if they are seated or standing many yards from the handset.

That's all there is to the amplifier situation, except that cheap ones give distorted, garbled messages.

The descriptions listed below, and the illustrations in figure 27, from the accessory auto-dialer to all-in-one units (telephone, auto-dialer/redialer, and amplifier), will give you some basic facts to work from in selecting your system. As usual, each will be delivered with a routine, two-wire, modular jack. Simply plug it into a duplex socket at your telephone (or add it into the lumpy clump you decided on instead) and it'll all start working.

$50 UNIT

- AN ADD-ON, STORES 16 TO 30 NUMBERS OF 7 TO 15 DIGITS.
- IT ONLY DIALS. YOU MUST HAVE AN ADJOINING TELEPHONE.
- IT MAY NOT HAVE AN INTERNAL BATTERY TO RETAIN YOUR STORED NUMBERS IF YOU DECIDE TO MOVE YOUR PHONE.

$75 UNIT

- OPTIONAL ON THE FOREGOING.

- WILL STORE 30 OR MORE NUMBERS, EACH 15 DIGITS OR MORE IF NEEDED.
- PERMITS "ON-HOOK" DIALING OF YOUR PHONE.
- HAS A FACE PLATE THAT WILL INDICATE NUMBERS BEING DIALED.
- HAS A BUILT-IN AMPLIFIER AS MONITOR AND SPEAKER.
- HAS A CLOCK AND CALL-TIMER FEATURE.
- REDIALER.
- BATTERY TO RETAIN MEMORY UNITS.

$125 UNIT

- HAS ALL THE FEATURES OF $100 UNIT *plus*—
- IT COMES COMPLETE WITH A BUILT-IN TELEPHONE.
- A "PRIVACY" BUTTON ENABLES YOU TO TURN OFF YOUR TELEPHONE MOUTHPIECE SO OTHER PARTY CAN'T HEAR CONVERSATIONS HAPPENING AT YOUR END OF THE CALL.
- "FEATHER-TOUCH" BUTTONS ENABLE THE MOST CASUAL OF OPERATING CONDITIONS.

Will the unit save you time in home or office? Yes.
Will it prove handy in an emergency? Yes. One button to

27 / AUTOMATIC DIALER/REDIALER TOP OF THE LINE

reach your doctor, hospital, or fire department could be handy and the auto-dialer won't dial incorrectly.

Is it worth the money for redial? Perhaps. Remember, however, the continual redialing is tying up your main trunk line.

Some auto-dialer units will work on multiline systems. An extra adapter must be purchased, however.

USED AUTO-DIALERS

As with telephone answering machines, your best bet is to see and hear them in operation before laying out your hard cash for used auto-dialers.

There are contacts and transistors within the units. If they've been dropped a few times or operated in high-humidity conditions, they might become balky and difficult, even worthless.

There is no easy way to test a used instrument without first plugging or wiring it into a working system. In a store, it's easy. At a garage sale it's more difficult. At a large outdoor swap meet, it's virtually impossible unless you can work out some kind of money-back deal with the seller and get assurance you'll meet again if the equipment proves to be less than advertised.

The other alternative is to order the unit from your local telephone company and pay approximately $10 a month extra for the service and equipment.

You know the retail selling prices of some of the units. You can estimate their manufacturing charges at less than a quarter of retail. Then decide for yourself which way is the best way for you to go. Into the auto-dialer/redialer accessory? Or a total telephone unit, complete with the "whole works?"

And will you rent it, or buy it from your local phone company, or buy it from another source?

Decisions, decisions. But aren't they fun?

BOTTOM LINE

As for the whole business of auto-dialers, I am of the opinion that there's merit in buying separate systems. By lumping memory systems, lights, buttons, loudspeakers, etc., into the same "container" with our basic telephone, we're inviting trouble. If any of the add-ons goes blooey, the phone goes out too, in many cases. You take your choice and your chances.

6 FANCY PHONES AND THINGS TO DO WITH THEM

The cordless portable pushbutton telephone will allow you to make or take your telephone calls in any room of your home or office, on the patio, or even while walking around the block, depending on pesky little problems that some buildings and other obstructions can cause.

The cordless telephone is a logical next step in telephone technology. The once-fictitious "wristwatch" telephone belonging to fictional Dick Tracy has arrived. The smallest models are still a bit too bulky for everyday wear on the wrist, but shirt-pocket models are already available and hand-held versions are everywhere, as you may have noticed. Let's review some of them, for better or worse, richer or poorer, and all that stuff.

FUNNY/FANCY/PHONES

We've discussed the fact that virtually all telephones are pretty much alike under the skin. Like people, they look different, but as every surgeon knows, the inner parts are similar and generally located in about the same old, dependable places.

It's fun and games to visit phone stores and see what's arrived since last month.

The Mickey Mouse® phone, the Snoopy® phone, the Decoy Duck phone—surely you've seen them, with price tags ranging $150 and up! I've heard that some of the marketing deals made on these items would baffle even the most unflappable lawyers.

Not long ago I saw my esteemed technical advisor for *Kiss Ma Bell Good-bye* removing the chime in a Decoy Duck phone to replace it with an electronic "Bow wow" to signal an incoming call. I couldn't howl "fowl" because I'd spent an entire day concealing the working parts of a telephone in an old shoe, positively my *last* experimental effort for a television network executive. He gets a vicarious kick out of picking up the old shoe when the phone "squeaks," talking into it, and dialing out, particularly when there are guests in his office. Ten years ago such a device would have been illegal, unkempt, and probably unfunny, except that Don Adams was using a "shoe phone" on his network show, *Get Smart,* as a running gag.

My current catalogue from Hammacher Schlemmer & Company (147 East 57th Street, New York, NY 10022) lists a chiming Decoy Duck phone for $259, either rotary or tone— definitely a mallard!

The same company offers several telephone styles, including those with clocks, timers, and eavesdrop detectors, but in truth, such items are available virtually everywhere on the continent, wherever phones are sold!

The Sharper Image Company sends me regular catalogues featuring astonishing telephones and other lavish equipment for home and office. Their "straightest" offering may be the famous Extend-A-Phone with built-in speaker, a huge memory, single-button dialing, redialing, and everything except ice water—approximately $150. They have a $99 Cordless, by Cobra (which we'll discuss in a minute), but my favorite is their phone built into a transparent plastic container. You can see the innards of the phone, complete, even as you use it. Offbeat, but clever!

Sharper Image, located at 406 Jackson Street, San Francisco, CA 94111, also catalogues the Panasonic® Integrated Phone for $269. It includes an all-feature solid-state tone telephone plus a variety of other gadgets, among them an auto-dialer that stores ten of your most frequently called numbers, up to sixteen digits in each position. There's an extra bank of storage space for holding utility and credit card numbers. That's handy for those areas where the local phone company or department store has "bill-paying service." You dial the "bill-paying service" and punch in the amount they should forward to your telephone company, electric, water, and gas utilities, and any other vendors you've listed. Deductions are made routinely from your bank account and the bills are paid, including the one for the bill-paying service, usually about $5–$12 a month, all by electronic beeps! Not a word or name need be mentioned.

The same phone gives you a choice of pulse or tone dialing, on-hook dialing, speakerphone, and automatic answering. You can carry your remote control unit and the phone will respond to your call from anywhere in the world and tell you who called while you were out. Naturally, there's a security code to prevent strangers from invading your answering unit.

TECHNOLOGY CONTINUED

The same telephone has a battery circuit to hold your memorized numbers in position if you move the phone from one modular jack to another plug-in socket. There are LED (light-emitting diode) indicator lights, soft/hard touch controls, instant erase, and other features that might be considered over-kill.

SUPER-GADGET

The Japanese manufacturers have included a unique feature in this model. Let's say you've set the machine to record incoming calls after the third ring. Then you travel overseas with your remote checker in your luggage. You can dial home with beeps from your remote gadget, but your machine won't answer until after the fifth ring if there are no messages to convey to you. You save the long-distance toll charges by hanging up after the fourth ring.

That's Panasonic's entry. Other manufacturers of quality can show you super-models that include radios which automatically lower the volume when you pick up the phone, tell you the length of each call you make, record the numbers you dial outside of your free-call area, and check for electronic "bugs." I use the extra word, "electronic," because in an earlier edition of the book I'd simply said "bugs," and a *Kiss Ma Bell Good-bye* reader wrote me at great length about her certainty that the new phone system was somehow causing her an endless series of cockroach and flea infestations!

Frankly, such multipurpose phones do not attract me personally, only because the failure of any one part makes it necessary to remove the whole unit for a ten-day or month-long repair job. It's a matter of personal choice. For myself, I prefer separate components. The other, more perfectionist member of our family duo likes everything in tidy packages. Hence, we have a stereo/radio/record player/reel tape player and cassette player, the cabinetry of solid oak, eight feet in length, complete with a marble top that requires three sumo wrestlers or a small forklift truck to move for dusting or semiannual shift-around of the household. As I say, it's a matter of personal choice—*yours*.

THE BOTTOM LINE ON WIRED PHONES

When divestiture was under way during 1983 and '84, most local phone companies were inviting their customers to (a) continue renting their telephones or (b) buy them through routine monthly installments, usually totalling $39.95 for everyday rotaries. Imagine the galvanized gall of dear old Ma. Say she'd installed a single rotary phone in your residence twenty years ago and charged you (at that time) about $15 for the hook-up. Then you started paying, say $1.50 a month, which was buried or "bundled" into your basic service charge. Not too many folks knew they were renting their phones in those days. For 240 months you paid, maybe $6–$8 a month for the dial tone *plus* $1.50 for that phone rental. Ma collected 240 times $1.50—$360, for a phone which two decades ago would have cost $5 or $6 to construct, package, and deliver into storage at your local company. Now she was offering you the chance to buy it all over again—$400 total for a $5 unit! Any wonder why Ma Bell became the richest, biggest business on the globe?

TH-TH-THERE'S M-M-MORE, F-F-FOLKS

If you'd had a Princess® model, the charge was probably about $5 a month—$1,200 rental fees for the phone set, which wasn't much from Day One. It was so light, it had to be held with one hand and dialed with the other, or else it would slide across a table top during the dialing process! After renting out a few hundred thousand of the things, Bell Labs told Western Electric to make the bases heavier—one of Ma's very few recalls. The auto makers should be so good!

So, you see, Ma Bell is both a saint and a sinner. And she's not likely to act "born again" now that all the regulations over her have been removed. Nevertheless, it was the same Ma Bell who gave us such a great phone system, best in the world. Why not? At the rates we were paying and the profits she was making, what should we expect?

BUT WHAT DO YOU EXPECT?

I shall not recommend any brand name or type of phone to you. You will probably get what you pay for in today's mixed-up market. The Bell Company's Research Labs, which brought us so many extraordinary things, like the rotary-dialer, the transistor, and their Touch Tone® system of dialing and switching, released very few items that weren't tested relentlessly (usually for five years minimum) before release to market. In the Los Angeles *Times* this week, a hardware store is selling imported phones called Tuch Tones (note the spelling) which will in truth access to the new long-distance services—at least a few times. They're selling for $6.66! I wouldn't hesitate to buy one and seal it in an airtight jar with a tiny package of silica gel (to absorb any moisture), to be used in an emergency. It's always possible that a good, solid phone will fail someday. A cheap spare just might get you through such a bad situation while you shop for a new, good instrument.

Competition is causing even some of our most distinguished producers of telephone equipment to move potentially less than perfect equipment into use—ITT, Automatic Electric, Western Electric, T.I.E., and Nippon Electric, to name a few of the "great ones."

I prefer a telephone with a solid, metal base, substantially hefty. Most new items these days are constructed of light plastic and untested components. I think my personal stock of old but good used instruments will serve me well.

Professional telephone installers working for the Big Seven companies usually load up about two or three times the number of sets their work orders for the day indicate. It's not unusual for the cheaper companies' installers to run through two, three, or more brand-new instruments before finding a good one when they're installing them for new customers!

WIRELESS TELEPHONES

Cobra® Company's Wireless Telephone is emerging as among the best of the "wireless" instruments. There are many brands, particularly Freedom, Nippon, Fanon, and the Ma Bell series, which are top quality. Each has a "receiver-transmitter" that walks with you, the message going back to the in-house, working base of the phone. The base unit, as in most present-day cordless phones, requires two attachments.

The standard modular connector snaps into the standard modular socket. Now, however, there'll be an additional electrical plug to snap into the standard 120-volt outlet. The purpose of the second connection is to supply some additional voltage for the transmitter in the base unit and also to provide charging current for the cordless extension handset, which snaps into charging position on the base when not in use.

This unit allows the user to take calls in any room of the house or nearby garage, even while walking along nearby streets. The range of most units taking incoming calls in this price range of $100 to $125 averages 600 feet, depending on how many steel-framed buildings and parked cars are between the base unit and the handset. For an additional $100 the cordless equipment will come equipped with a dial-out feature.

The Freedom phone, mentioned earlier, is foremost in breaking through the biggest problem with wireless phones. Freedom 4000 is the state of the art model for wireless phone users who have been horrified by interference, static, and breakdown. *Don't let the technical words bother you—please! Most cordless phones transmit their signal from the transmitter (mouthpiece) in the handset back to the phone's base unit on a 49-MHz carrier frequency. The signal (voice) returning from the base to the handset (earpiece) locked in on 1.7 MHz. That's been responsible for lots of wireless phones being tossed into trash compactors. Freedom Phone company uses the 49 MHz frequency going both ways. The result in most (perhaps 95* percent) of all locations has become almost as good as wired phones. In addition, Freedom has tossed in pulse as well as tone, emergency or instant-calling buttons—even a six-digit security code that can be jiggered around to shut out all other cordless phones in the area. U.S.-built. Lots of other features. If it's worth $249 to you, call Sharper Image—they will accept your credit card order at toll-free 800-344-4444. In Canada, 415-344-4444. If you don't think it's for you after trying it for a couple of weeks, send it back for a refund.

The wireless phones all look pretty much the same.

The unit pictured in figure 28 represents the current state of the art in standard-size phone units. The instrument is available in both rotary and pushbutton models. Its connection methods are the same as the "incoming only" receiver. It's a full duplex system, enabling simultaneous conversation capability, no need to "push-to-talk, release-to-hear" as the earliest walkie-talkie systems demanded. The Fanon Courier® claims FM quality, distortion-free, quiet operation. So do most other top-quality labels. Maybe so.

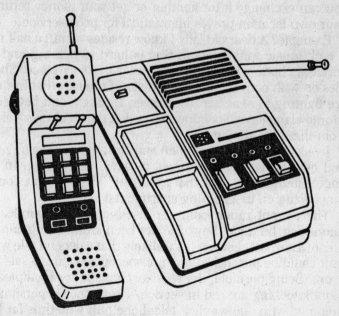

28 / WIRELESS TELEPHONE STATE OF THE ART

Power is supplied in the portable handset by rechargeable nickel-cadmium batteries. Whenever the handset is dropped into the rest position in the base, two connectors interlock automatically with base sockets to carry on the charging of the batteries. The handset is equipped with a tiny indicator light (a light-emitting diode), which lets the user know when battery recharging time is approaching.

An additional feature not available in all cordless units is the "hi-lo" volume control, which can be handy if Dad is making a phone call while hunched over the roaring engine of a car in the garage.

At time of publication, the unit pictured was retailing for $225 at most electronic distributors.

Most portable no-cord telephones, even the costly models, are still subject to immense problems of interference. Local radio and TV stations can often be heard in the background of conversations. Static, sputtering, and break-up of signals often turn wireless phones into objects of frustrating annoyance. Never, but never, buy a cordless unit without getting a guarantee that you can exchange it for another or get your money returned if your own location proves impractical for good service.

Example? A dear old lady I know resides within a half mile of a rock music radio station. She is hard of hearing and has a wireless phone with a hefty amplifier in its earpiece. She babbles on with conversations, heedless of the fact that her callers are fighting to hear her words over, through, and between the thump-clang-smash-commercial racket that is always leaking in from the radio station.

I've heard of units that open and close electrical garage doors and others that cause animals to howl wildly when in use. I once listened to a unit that "bugged" all the other conversations going on in adjoining apartments!

There's not much point in discussing used wireless telephone sets because they have not been around long enough to create a surplus market. It's unlikely that a dependable wireless unit could be purchased at a nonspecialized garage sale in any event. Being portable, the receiver/transmitter handpiece gets more knocking around in service. The author is personally acquainted with one wireless telephone buff who thus far has replaced four, count 'em, four handsets.

Number one was lost after he was using it to hold a conversation with *me* while he was working under his automobile. He "hung it up" when we'd concluded our chat and shortly thereafter drove over the poor thing.

Number two was dropped into a bathtub of water.

Number three simply disappeared. We both suspect he "hung it up" in the garbage pail in the kitchen.

Number four proved to have an internal malfunction. I suspect it was the crystal control that was supposed to hold the handset on its designated frequency. After four recalls to his friendly phone shop, the decision was made to replace it entirely with a new unit.

The wife of a neighbor carries her handset with her whenever she goes out to jog or walk her dog. Her husband, who works in his residence, has a separate "business line," which he switches to hands-off amplifier whenever she goes out for after-dark runs.

She dials their "business number" upon leaving the house and keeps up a running commentary to her husband (pardon the pun) while she's out alone in the dark of night.

"It's a real handy gadget," says my friend. "Not too long ago a cruising car pulled up alongside her. She described the action, and I was making a dash for the front door before she told me to keep calm and stay home. Just the appearance of the handset and a message being delivered was enough to send the mobile masher on his way with tires screeching!"*

As this book is being readied for press, a local electronics store is offering a brand-new, high-quality wireless telephone with pushbuttons, on sale, for $59. Brand-new? High-quality? Pushbuttons? $59? It's an unlikely possibility. This type of ad may trip up the unwary buyer. Maybe it's a bait-and-switch attraction. Personally, I think I'll wait for the $250 unit to go on sale for $199.95. But even then, with wireless equipment, I'll insist on a *money-back guarantee*. No exchanges! Strictly money-back, no questions asked, if the phone doesn't work well in my geographic location.

---

*If you have an old, nonworking handpiece, rig it up with a coat hanger "antenna" (12″ long) and carry it with you on neighborhood walks, as a sham "protection device."

7 TELEPHONES ON WHEELS AND IN BOXES— THE CELLULAR SYSTEM OF WIRELESS PHONES

You may have observed people doing unusual things while driving their cars. Women will be seen adjusting their makeup. Men will drive while shaving, with their razors plugged into the cigarette lighter socket. If you're like me, when you see such things, you might shake your head and ask, "What's this world coming to?"

Do you feel the same when you observe drivers skimming through traffic with a telephone pressed to an ear? Less likely. We've become used to the phenomenon, dangerous as it is. Here and now I'll make a prediction! Before long, it'll be against the law for the driver of an automobile to make a phone call while the vehicle is in motion. And companies will be springing up to sell speakerphones or hidden-in-the-ear devices to defeat the law. That's the American way! In fact, suitable gadgets are here already. If I had a cellular telephone, I'd equip it with a speakerphone to eliminate the handset and add the "audio" feature which enables a caller to simply bellow the name of the person to be called. The phone hears and dials the number for you. We'll talk about all these things as we progress. I've delayed making my own cellular purchase for reasons mentioned later in this chapter.

Should passengers make phone calls? Sure. Why not? But drivers should be required to stop and park before phoning. The business of phones in cars, heralded as something sensational—the business of the future—is doing well and shows signs of improvement. When cellular phone systems first hit the market, they looked like solid-gold investments. Well, if you'd been one of the gate-crashers to pick up, say, 1,000 shares of Communications Systems, Inc., at $40, your $40,000 worth would have been valued at about $17,500 a couple of months later. The cellular business was oversold. Only now is it making steady progress. The fast-buck crowd has been forced out. The dependable suppliers and installers are making a great idea work better each day.

PHONES ON WHEELS

Because of the general retardation of the Federal Communications Commission (FCC), combined with Ma Bell's monopoly of the telephone business, car telephones were a scrungy proposition when the AT&T lawyers caved in, on cue, to the demands of the Justice Department on January 8, 1982. Remember, only Ma Bell herself could put a phone in your car at that point in time. It wasn't much of a deal. Let's flash back, as they do in the movies.

FADE IN: ANY DAY IN TWO BIG CITIES, 1978–1982 PERIOD

There were about 700 cars in New York equipped with telephones, about 7,500 in Los Angeles. But the New York Telephone System had fewer than twenty-five "lines" (more accurately called "dedicated frequencies") to be shared by the 700 customers. And out west, in Los Angeles, Pacific Bell with nearby General had fewer than a hundred lines set up for their 7,500 overanxious wheeler-spielers.

Ma Bell had been holding back on the new system, given the name "cellular," that she'd invented in 1946.. After making sure nobody else could get rights to the system, Ma showed it to the FCC, which sat on it from 1964 through 1971, about three years before the Justice Department would come crashing down on both the FCC and AT&T with an antitrust suit. It must have jarred the poor old FCC. As for Ma Bell, she's never caught napping.

THE OLD SYSTEM—WHICH HAD ITS PROBLEMS

Under the old rules, Ma Bell had been given the people's air space to sell for car telephones. Mini–radio stations were stuffed into the trunks of cars. The units were alleged to be capable of reaching fifty miles in all directions to contact a central, mobile phone office that could "patch" the car buff to home or business, long distance, even to another car. A quick call might cost $10, to say nothing of the $4,000 costs of installation and annual maintenance. The conversations were crackly with static, if intelligible at all.

THE NEW SYSTEM—WHICH IS BEGINNING TO SOUND GREAT

Ma Bell's new idea in 1946 was to reduce each area to be covered. The various market areas would be honeycombed into "cells" that could pick up and reamplify and relay calls in short jumps to the central offices, where the connections could continue via copper wires on poles, or microwave, or satellite, or whatever! After divestiture, hundreds of companies scrambled into the business, and thousands of subscribers succumbed to alluring advertisements of installations "as cheap as $1,500 to $2,000." Nothing was ever said about the $25 monthly charge for "access to the phone company" or 50 cents a minute while you were talking. The voice quality wasn't much better than the old system, at first.

Except for the advantages of enabling more people to spend more money for more phones in more cars, cellular systems in '82 and '83 held little promise until they improved in quality and came down in price. Even today, there's room for improvement on both counts.

Near the end of 1984, Western Union was advertising its own mobile telephone, saying it would work as well as your telephone at home or office. It was a cinch to have installed. Drive, push buttons, and talk to anybody, anywhere, particularly if you told your local company to hook into Western Union's long-distance facilities. Now, really! If many providers are involved in giving you a faulty phone call, who'll be to blame? The phone maker? The car manufacturer? The phone company? The outfit that installed the cellular amplifier? The computer? The unit itself? The long-distance service? Take care. The units can be rigged to perform admirably in ideal circumstances. Don't be misled by "setup" demonstrations.

If you get into a cellular deal, try to get a minimum of ten-days cash refund if it doesn't satisfy you perfectly in the places you drive. And that refund should include the installation and removal charge *plus* a rubber plug to conceal the antenna hole that'll be drilled through your car's body. Don't settle for "exchanges." If you can't be guaranteed a money-back, speedy service contract, walk away from the promoter.

ELECTRONIC VOODOO

You'd really have to examine a detailed drawing of "cellular" to see why it's a good idea, almost beyond our technological know-how. The exciting process of picking up your car phone and dialing anywhere in the world to send your voice jazzing around by computer from "cell" to "cell" without hearing clicks, clacks, static, and disconnects is almost beyond belief.

Some communities, blessed by their topography and patience, have superb cellular systems. One system in the U.S.A. has been operating for a quarter century, though it's not really Ma Bell's cellular scheme. In Long Beach, California, years ago, licensed radio amateurs set up only five "cell-type" amplifiers, strategically located, for their police. Police units could move about freely within that system, which is still in use. If a police car passed behind a tall steel building, the amplifier transmitter/receiver serving the car would be interrupted but another location would take over, instantaneously adjusting the signal strength until the moving vehicle returned to a more convenient location and the original amplifier or yet another continued the signal. The messages back and forth from the police cars to headquarters and among the cars themselves would move along without interruption—with only those five homemade gadgets. A comparable cellular system in such an area might require fifty cells to get the same result. But let's not forget, the police system doesn't network into the telephone system, though it could be made compatible, I'm told.

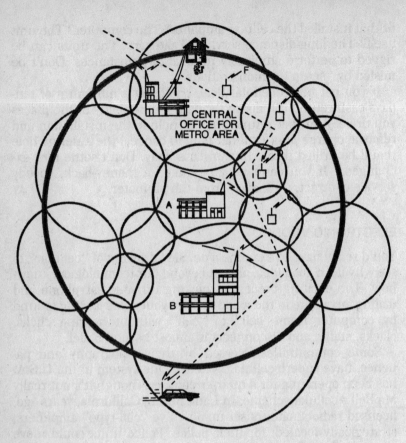

29 / CELLULAR SYSTEM REMOTE TELEPHONING

The cellular concept, from Ma Bell in '46, reached the FCC electronic geniuses a few years later. A 75-MHz band (806 to 881) was set aside for cellular, and research was begun. The Institute of Electrical and Electronics Engineers, Inc., the elite of the radio amateurs and professional wizards, set up a special group on Vehicular Technology and began documenting everything known about the technique. In their 244-page magazine of November 1973, they described the theory. I've read that report a dozen times and am not only awed by the circuitry, but convinced that it is more complicated than anything else in tele-communications today. And yet in this morning's paper, there were many companies in Los Angeles promoting cellular tele-phone systems—installed in 2 to 3 hours for ONLY $1,995.00. (Prices varied, from $1,000 to $2,500.) I recall that in mid-1984 I talked to some cellular supervisors for the area's phone ser-vices. They told me there'd been so much experimenting going on with cellular amplifiers over the years that they had lost all record of their locations, but many of them were still function-ing. They'd been squirreled away and turned on in closets, on rooftops, wherever they could operate without being readily seen, and were operating a decade later! Company search teams located them soon thereafter.

I can only wish the buyers and the sellers lots of luck in their enthusiasm. Make no mistake. Excellent cellular systems are available for purchase today. Installed with precision they can be practical, though expensive.

It would be pleasant to call home on the way to or from the office, to pass along an important message or hear that certain special voice. Well-installed systems today, right now, are miles ahead of the old method. Three years hence the process should indeed be as good as a home-wired telephone—workable, prac-tical, and dependable. Right now, a cheap, badly installed sys-tem will cause a cellular chat to be more annoying than listening to Howard Cossell reading *Hamlet* or interpreting a shopping list.

BUYING AT WHOLESALE

If you simply must have a car telephone and you can write off its cost on your income tax, look in the want ads of your local paper in any of the thirty largest city areas where cellular has been available since 1983. Almost invariably, the present owner will state that his or her system is less than a month old and will be happy to unload it on you at a $400–$500 loss. It's not hard to guess why. The cheap models, even expensive ones that are shabbily installed, are often a disappointment. I heard of one car/phone buff who bought a new $12,000 car and had a $2,-500 phone installed without a penny of down payment on either. He drove it for two weeks before both car and equipment were stolen. After the insurance coverage, less the deductible amounts, he'll be paying $200 a month for eighteen months. That car, reconsidered, will have cost him $10 a mile (he'd driven 200 miles) and $300 a call (he'd made three of them) before the whole mess was swiped. If you need credit, you don't need a telephone in your car. Let's put it that way, okay?

The idea of cellular telephones is good, but the execution is often bad. The last hands-on exhibition I saw enabled me to spend a nine-hour day watching skilled technicians installing several different brand names in as many cars. The shortest time was two hours; the longest, eight hours. And many of the telephones on wheels stuttered, sputtered, garbled and gurgled, snapped, crackled, and popped, most of them in the parking area of the local telephone company! Eventually they were all made to work perfectly. On a test run, we were told we'd passed through five cells without even a hint of static or switch click. The level of the ongoing conversation didn't vary a spit, and there was perfect voice quality during our four-mile excursion.

There are three vitally important aspects of any cellular telephone function, which all add up to this: You get what you pay for, after knowing what you're buying.

1. The mobile unit must be made with precision to withstand the shaking, bumping, sparking, direction-changing characteristics of the vehicle in which it's installed.

2. The master computer of the regional phone company and all of its "cellular amplifier locations" must be engineered to accommodate messages from any point to any point in the area being served. And the equipment must be able to measure signal strengths in billionths of a second, transferring from one amplifier to the next without a tweak of static, interruption, or hash. And remember, the nature of all locations is changing, virtually hourly. Traffic loads, weather, types of factory activity in the area of each amplifier, even the erection or removal of billboards can be vitally important to the operation of good cellular systems. You will be dealing with at least three different contractors—the equipment manufacturer, the installer, and

the phone company. Before you spend a penny, make sure you get satisfactory responses about guarantees and quality from each of the three.

3. The *single most important* factor in a good cellular phone setup is the installation of the unit within the vehicle. It's essential that it be done by a formally licensed technician, with top-of-the-line recommendations. The day may come when this will be a do-it-yourself process. Right now, it would be a foolish project for most amateurs. The exotic equipment needed to tune the phone to the vehicle and the assembly to the system is barely within the scope of even most telephone companies today. You may be surprised to learn that some, if not all, local phone companies are contracting their cellular installations out of the phone company, to be done by independent technicians with equipment worth tens of thousands of dollars and track records of proven skill.

CELLULAR THINGS ARE GETTING BETTER BY THE DAY

With names like Motorola, General Electric, Tandy, Oki, Nippon Electric (NEC) (Japan), and Ericsson (Sweden) out to grab the huge market, in collaboration with the Seven Sisters and major independent phone companies, cellular phone systems are improving daily.

Now that the rental car companies, Hertz, Avis, Budget, National, and others, will rent you cars with telephones in them (for about $10 a day extra, plus your time charges), the mobile phones will *have* to be as easy to operate and sound as good as business phones.

And the long-distance carriers, like MCI, Western Union, and ARGO, are in the act, demanding better equipment. The engineers are talking to themselves. After all, cars are complex and wildly thrashing combinations of gears, wheels, electrical sparking, and noisy bearings. It's inevitable that moving automobiles themselves louse up some equipment that works beautifully when sitting on the assembly bench.

Let's examine what the experts' expert has said and is saying about cellular. These decrees are all from Lehmann Brothers Kuhn Loeb, investment specialists whose words can unlatch money forces worldwide.

In 1982 they said that in Southern California alone there were 278,000 customers panting to get car telephones on the new cellular system. Not so, as things turned out.

In 1983 they said the market in cellular phones was "berserk." I conclude that's a synonym for "don't know."

In 1984 they commented that cellular "is a generally depressed market." That was a borderline fact. Actually, it was a shake-out year. The opportunists were exposed. The cellular system was beginning to be understood and made to work by licensed experts. The bums were being tossed out of the game. So much for the crystal-ball gazers.

A year later they were still not predicting for '86.

And remember, these are the specialists, people who charge huge sums for such extraordinary commentaries. The only fact I can glean is that the expert installers (and there aren't many of them) did exceedingly well in '84. One of them estimated that he'd had about 15 percent of all units returned for major adjustment and about a third of those were ordered removed by the owners. The other installers made no comments on their customers' responses beyond saying, "They're happy with their new toys." Boys and girls will be big, happy kids at any price, I suppose.

ANOTHER PRECINCT HEARD FROM

Fortune magazine stated in their August 6, 1984, edition that by 1990 the number of phones on wheels could be expected to approach 700,000, enough to produce revenues of $1.3 billion a year. Then, immediately, they added their inevitable "but." They wrote, "But that may be a modest estimate, based on the probably faulty assumption that costs will stay as they are rather than fall. Industry experts think lower rates—and rising demand—are certain." (If anyone can tell me what that all means, I'd appreciate the advice.) At least it may give you an idea of how limited we tend to be in matters of cellular certainties. If you want a cellular telephone in your car and if you can afford it painlessly, go for it. Settle for nothing but the *best*. And don't lose or misplace your guarantees. Shop around. It's not the type of thing to buy in the dark. And skip the stolen items. They're quite easy to trace when you ask your phone company to give you access.

THE BETTER IDEA FOR CELLULAR

In my opinion, the mobile telephone, as it stands today, is well beyond the gimmick stage. It will not end up like CB radio, which fell flat on its megacycles very quickly because of its static, interference, and general polluting effect on our senses.

Undoubtedly, mobile phones of high quality, skillfully installed and adequately powered, say, 5 watts minimum output, will remain in demand. And in most cases, their hefty costs will be paid by us small taxpayers because the big wheels of industry with unlimited expense accounts will write them off as business deductions.

Word is getting out as this edition of *Kiss Ma Bell Good-bye* goes to press that Radio Shack (Tandy) stores are ready to let the "ordinary fellow" into the field with a home-installed mobile phone (cellular system) eventually to sell for less than $1,000. That may be the breakthrough, if the things work well. Then the phone companies will have to get precise about cellular, multiply the availability of lines, and get hustling to keep the system popular enough to be a profitable service. A complicated chain of events, eh?

If I had to make a guess, I'd bet the GE, Motorola, or Nippon Electric, maybe Northern Telcom, will come up with cellular telephone rigs that people can rely on, can use without getting ulcers, and can afford.

TOUCH OF TECHNOLOGY

When the cellular system does catch on, its expansion capability is built into the system. The basic amplifiers which relay the phone callers' messages via master computers from cell to adjoining cell to adjoining cell to the other correspondent each has an initial capacity of about 650 simultaneous calls. When the number of users increases, when the load of calls exceeds the availability of any cell, the phone companies will simply be required to divide the overloaded unit into halves, fire up an extra amplifier/switcher nearby, pray a little, and continue on, merrily making money for their investors and a better telecommunications system for the talkers.

In super-dense locations like the World Trade Center in New York, the Wrigley complex in Chicago, or the hub of Los Angeles, an extra cell or two or more could be added, overnight, if and when needed. Some buildings may require one or two separate cells of their very own if business is high-volume.

So the idea is good, the present state of the art is encouraging, and the future should be bright.

ONE ASSURANCE OF CELLULAR'S SUCCESS

There is one superb idea that will virtually guarantee the success of cellular telephone. A *portable* unit in a box, a briefcase, or purse, small, compact, and clear of quality in voice or data transmission. I am tempted to buy one. I can carry it wherever I go and even make calls from my car. And I can carry it with me from my car, making the vehicle less attractive to burglars. There are such units available right now, somewhat limited in their range and susceptible to interference. We will soon see available, I'm *certain*, units that can pump out as much as 5 watts of FM power from lightweight, rechargeable batteries. They will go anywhere that you can travel and make a connection from a pushbutton pad, from any location, to any other. The call charges will be expensive but, for the user, perhaps worth it. Intensive competition is the very thing that divestiture was meant to stimulate. It's going to chase out the bad guys and reward the good ones.

8 GIMMICKS, GADGETS, AND GIGO

TELEPHONE GADGETRY

- In the area of gadgetry, I think the Porta-Touch, made by Buscom Electric, is unique. Weighing 3 ounces, it's like a slice of a base-ball. You'd hardly notice the weight of it in pocket or purse. It's a miniature memory dialer that is held close to any phone receiver. Press two buttons for Mom, the office, your best customer—as many as forty VIPs in your life—and the connection's made fast. Seventy-five dollars, via Sharper Image, page 99. Also, the unit will pushbutton (tone) unmemorized numbers.

- The same company will supply you with Soft Touch. It simply screws on as a replacement mouthpiece for your present phone, the buttons "built in." With forty regular numbers in its memory, it too will dial new numbers and is workable on the long-distance services. Also $75, same supplier as above.

- The Electronic Phone Book is a miniature computer, smaller and much lighter than a pack of playing cards, that'll let you punch in up to sixty-three names and phone numbers and dial any one you want by holding it against the phone transmitter. It requires seven watch batteries for long-lasting power, but at $199 you may want to order it, same supplier as above.

- The Jumbo Button phone is available at the same location, made by Webcor. The handset fits onto the pushbutton pad, which is bigger than a cigar box, each digit on the phone as big as four sugar cubes. It would be an ideal gadget for people with vision problems or very fat fingers. Most phone company stores stock them or reasonable facsimiles in the vicinity of $100. Variety stores have slightly smaller versions of touch pads that simply sit on your regular touch pad phone. But the numbers look about three times bigger than normal. Prices run upwards to $15 for such accessories.

- Phone Tap is a small box that plugs into your modular socket, your telephone into the box. Also there's a socket on the box into which you can plug your tape recorder. It's all automatic, turning itself on and off only when the line is being used. Also, *it is an illegal device, if used incorrectly.*

The phone tap laws are vague, but here they are. If *one* of the parties to a conversation knows the phone call is being recorded, it's legal, even if the knowing person is *you*, the phone tapper. It's flat out illegal if neither party to a chat knows there's a recording being made. Don't bug your phone on the babysitter. If he or she finds out, you can be sued to you-know-where. And of course it's a very definite no-no to tap or tape record anything on a party line. Nevertheless, DAK Industries of 10845 Vanowen Street in North Hollywood, CA 91605 (or toll-free 800-325-0800), will sell you a Phone Tap for $22.50.

The same firm and many others across the country will be happy to sell you other telephone gadgets, including:

- THE IMPOSTER.   About $75, it's a special handset to *replace* the one on your present telephone base. The unit "stores" every number you wish, as you dial it the first time, up to eighty-three total sets of numbers. It features a volume control and amplifer. It'll plug into many brands of office, multiline handsets, too.

- TWO-LINE BREAKTHROUGH.   At $69, DAK's Thinfone® is probably the world's cheapest (to date) two-line phone unit. If you have two lines entering your residence, you can answer or call out on either, through the single handset and dialer that has "hold" and lots of bells, buttons, lights, and beepers. Manufacturer unspecified.

- ILLEGAL PHONE.   The same company will sell you their wireless, super-strength phone, which the FCC may zap off the market during 1986 or earlier. It's overpowered, for a range of up to 1,500 feet. As of mid-1985 it's waivered as okay by the FCC. It has a ten-number memory, made by Universal Security Instrument Company. One hundred and nine dollars. Lots of other goodies on it, too!

- VOICE PRINT ANSWERER.   DAK'S oddest gadget this time around is an answering machine. It does all the things that most phone answering machines do plus it requires no remote beeper if you call home for messages. In fact, the machine will beep you twice it it recognizes your voice and wants to tell you there's no message on your recorder. If the answerer is loaded, it'll deliver the messages and then beep five times to advise that it has delivered all its news. It's a Unitech Instrument, generally considered a quality product. It records conversations between two parties, too. It has a half dozen extra gimmicky features. $159 plus tax and postage—or shop your specialty stores.

- SPEAKERPHONE. A DAK special—$29. Plug it in with a double connector at your modular socket and you can talk and listen while you do your aerobics.

- CHEAP WIRELESS PHONES.   They are available everywhere, from every supplier, at incredibly low or high prices. It seems to me that a person would be foolish to pay any amount less than $150 for a wireless phone. It's either stolen or worthless. It'll drive you silly with static, and it may well cause you some embarrassment. Read on . . .

THE WIRELESS PHONE SURPRISE

In case you didn't know, when you talk on a wireless phone, almost any neighbor will be able to hear both sides of your conversation if his/her AM radio is turned on or he/she happens to pick up his/her own wireless phone. Unitech (via your local store or DAK) has come up with a gimmicky security system to let you punch in one set from among 512 different sets of numbers of exclude nearby wireless telephones.

Frankly, I can't see how you'll ever be *sure* your wireless unit is off limits to all neighbors, but if you figure it out, let me know! The Split Personality Unit (as they call it), described above, sells for $99. It might work. I don't know.

- NUMB EAR MIRACLE.   That's what DAK calls its over-the-head talk-hearphone. It's a cheap copy of the units used by telephone operators. Forty-nine dollars. The unit I use is made by Plantronics, 345 Encinal Street, Santa Cruz, CA 95060. Their "Star Set" model is more expensive—it's the professional unit with ultra-fidelity. But when there are long interviews or conversations, they're the greatest thing to wear, freeing up both hands, enabling the user to write without bending his or her head weirdly to hold the telephone in position.

Why shouldn't I confess right here that a few months ago, while engaged in a two-hour radio talk show about another book, I chatted with the announcer and telephone callers throughout the Midwest while refinishing my typewriter table. Try doing *that* while holding a phone receiver with no hands!

BUZZERS

If, when you did your initial wiring (or used existing lines), you discovered four conductors or more in the cabling, you can readily wire in a pushbutton buzzer at each phone location, as shown in figure 30. Two of the spare conductors can be used to install a simple pushbutton and buzzer on each phone. Each member of the household can be assigned a number of buzzes as identification. No matter who answers any phone, a sequence of buzzes will summon the correct individual to pick up on the nearest extension.

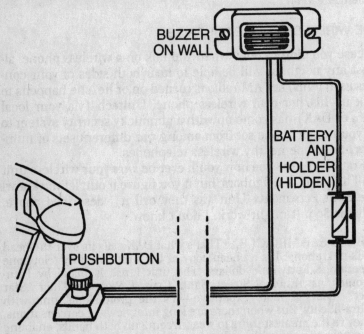

30 / BUZZER CIRCUIT OLD-FASHIONED BUT DEPENDABLE

THE PHONE BELL

The material in this book has frequently made reference to the phone bell "ringer" or just plain "bell." Clanging bell sounds are speedily being replaced by beeps, bloops, ding-dongs, and even one device which plays a different song with each incoming call. An old friend of mine from the Deep South has had me change his telephone bell into a banjo rendition of "Dixie." Regrettably, the first time around I set his machine up to play the first sixteen bars of his song. It became the rough equivalent of

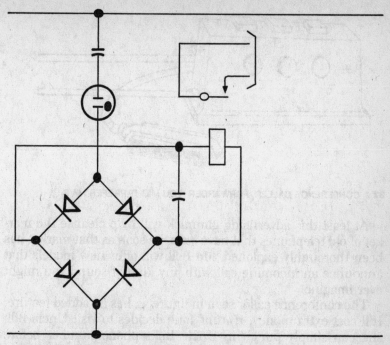

31 / ADD A CHIME, ADD ANYTHING   A COVER-ALL CIRCUIT

waiting for five rings every time I called him, because he could never bring himself to lift the receiver before hearing all the music. I cut him back to the first four bars out of self-defense.

And this information may have bearing on the reasons why many of the cast-adrift Bell Telephone companies are now offering to let their subscribers *buy* the telephones already installed in their homes.

For example, in Los Angeles, Pacific Bell Telephone offered all its subscribers the chance to buy their existing rotaries for $19, Princess® models for $27, and Trimlines® for $34. Each of the models in pushbutton style is available for approximately $15 additional. And payments can be made monthly.

Remember, for subscribers who have been using the phones for five to ten years, on lease, the deal means that they've already paid for the instrument any number of times. Now they can pay for them once more! One final chance, eh?

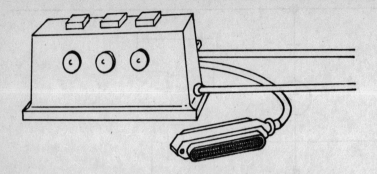

At least this advertising gimmick will help cleanse the market of old telephones that have *bells*. As soon as that market has been thoroughly exploited, Ma Bell will offer new models that announce an incoming call with any kind of sound you might ever imagine.

The conference caller seen in figure 32 has an added feature. It'll cost extra money. If Aunt Jane decides to visit Uncle Bill, she can simply punch in Uncle Bill's phone number before leaving her home and any calls made to her number will be forwarded along to her at Uncle Bill's, automatically.

Don't buy this equipment, however, before checking with your local telephone company. Progressive local companies can add this facility to your present phone line on a monthly rental basis. Early indications are that the cost will be modest, particu-

larly if the add-on can be done by a technician within the central office, without having to visit your home.

AMPLIFIERS

Consider buying an amplifier if there are hearing-impaired persons involved in your life. A simple amplifier such as shown in figure 33 will plug in, form a parallel circuit with the phone, and has a switch which enables the whole room to be filled with the sound of the incoming caller's voice. Any number of people can talk back and forth in a hands-off conference-style call although no telephones will be in use, assuming the incoming caller is similarly equipped.

For the hearing-impaired, you can install an amplifier-receiver without a "squawk box," as the loudspeakers are known. A small button on top of the handset enables the listener to turn the volume up or down on the receiver of the telephone.

When you talk through any ordinary telephone, a certain balanced amount of your call is simultaneously being heard through your earpiece. It's a "side-tone," in technical jargon.

But you may not appreciate it until you stifle the sound in your own earphone. You'll be surprised how eerie it sounds when you can't hear the sound of your own voice coming back through your earpiece as you speak. It'll give you an incentive to provide an amplifying handpiece for anyone you know who is hard of hearing.

POTPOURRI OF TELEPHONE ACCESSORIES

Telephone stores and phone shops run by Ma will offer you a bewildering assortment of interesting, if rather unnecessary, gadgetry for your telephone usage.

Switches are available to shut off the ringing sound altogether. Others are available that snap in place and make it easy to adjust the level without having to turn the set upside down and fumble for the bell control.

There are battery-driven indexes to list numbers and names and addresses. And you might enjoy having one of the many styles of clip-on things that enable you to rest the receiver against your shoulder while you use your hands for other work or play. And there are even solid-gold caps that clip over your handset to give a monogram ornamentation. Another gizmo that can be plugged in or simply stuck on to a handset will enable you to tape record conversations if you have a cassette recorder. A snap-on amplifier boosts the speaker's voice as much as five times normal. Another plastic attachment can be carried in your pocket but when clipped over a mouthpiece will tell you by visual signal if there is any "bug" on the line or if anyone else is eavesdropping on your conversation on an extension.

All of these are available right now at your friendly phone store.

THE CURRENT ULTIMATE ACCESSORY

The BSR X-10 system is the first mass-produced version of an accessory that has been operating on a homemade basis in the homes of telephone buffs for many years. Now, at last it's been refined to the point where anybody can own one and attach it in seconds to their residential phone system. The BSR system, or any of the multiple systems that have tried to do BSR's job cheaper, enables you to protect and control your home and all electromechanical devices within it from any telephone, anywhere in the world.

The X-10 unit seen in figure 34 is limited to eight basic control functions, but can readily be advanced to perform ninety-nine functions with a simple bit of reworking by any alert electronics technician.

In terms of your needs and wants, it may be the most exciting add-on that's entered the telephone field for many years.

The large unit is the base station that plugs into two sockets in your home. One plug is inserted in an electrical outlet, the other in our ever-popular telephone duplex jack. You decide which functions you'd like to control by telephone calls.

If you decide on telephoning the living room lamp, the radio, the TV/videocassette recorder, the microwave oven, you simply insert modules (supplied with the system) in the sockets where those items are now plugged, making note of which module is in which socket, controlling which appliance.

That's it! You're ready. You toss the tiny remote transmitter into your pocket and off you go to work or a trip around the world.

106

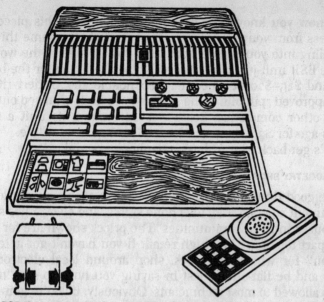

Let's suppose you have placed a module in your BSR X-10 that will enable you to reach your answering machine monitor. You've placed that module in position 4, let us say.

Later in the day, you dial your home. The answering machine responds and you hold your remote unit up to the telephone at your calling position and depress button 4.

For the next period of preset time, the answering machine monitor will deliver to you all the calls that reached your home during your absence. Dial position 5 and it'll cut in a microphone to relay anything happening at that minute in your house.

You can also arrange to have it report to you if any of the windows or doors have opened while you were away, because it's tied in to your home security system!

Before hanging up, you may decide to turn on the oven (push button 6), turn on the outdoor lights (button 8), and instruct the TV/videocassette recorder to tape a show.

The machine will signal you a positive note when these instructions have been received. You hang up and go on your way.

By now you know that if you can accomplish this piece of business from your office, you can do exactly the same things by dialing into your home from the opposite side of the world.

The BSR unit just described will cost about $90 for the base unit and $15–$20 per module. Dependable and Underwriters Lab–approved spin-offs of the system have been churned out by many other companies. Sears was advertising its unit a few weeks ago for $39 (base unit) and $10–$15 per module.

Let's get back to your basic telephone system!

THE GADGETRY SHOP

All the good things seen in figure 35 are available now at local department stores, radio/telephone stores, and electronics supply houses in most communities. The prices shown are for the most part top-of-the-line high retail. If you haven't got a "connection" for wholesale prices, shop around local electronics stores and be flat-out honest in saying you hope to get "net" prices allowed to most technicians. Obviously, if you're going to buy only one or two items, it won't be worth the effort. Let's see some of the components you might desire.

A. QUICK PLUG
CONVERTS OLD PHONES FOR MODULAR JACKS $2.50

B. DUPLEX JACK
ENABLES TWO JACKS TO ENTER ONE OUTLET 3.50

C. MODULAR SOCKET
A "TERMINAL SOCKET" FOR THE WALL 3.50

D. MOD-MOD CORDS
REPLACEMENT CORDS FOR YOUR PHONE: 7 FEET 3.00
12 FEET 4.00
25 FEET 6.00

E. IN-LINE COUPLERS
INTERCONNECTS 2 JACK PLUGS 2.50

F. PLUG ADAPTER
CONVERTS 4-PRONG TO MODULAR SOCKET 4.00

G. WALL PLATE
TO MAKE THE TERMINAL FLUSH TO WALL 5.00

H. EXTENSION CORDS
TO ADD LENGTH TO EXISTING CORDS 25 FEET 4.00

I. INSTANT JACK
CONVERTS 4-PRONG TO MODULAR JACK 3.50

108

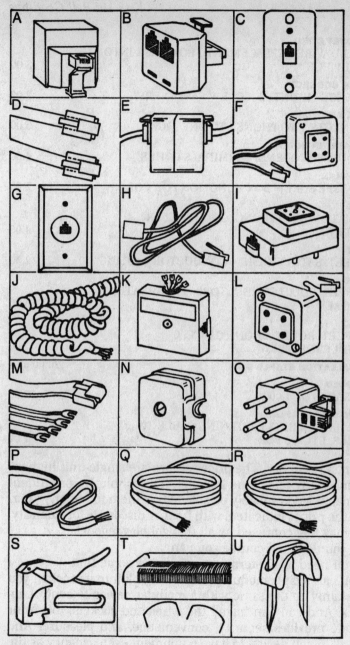

109

J. HANDSET CORD
COILED WIRE REPLACEMENT FROM BASE INTO
HANDPIECE   3.00

K. QUICK CONNECT
SURFACE MOUNTED, SCREW FASTENERS   3.00

L. JACK AND PLUG
CONNECTS TWO PHONES TO ONE JACK   5.00

M. CONVERTER CORD
MODULAR ONE END, TERMINALS OTHER   4.00

N. TERMINAL
OLD-TYPE SCREW BOX. JUNCTION FOR CORDS   2.00

O. PLUG
TO MATE WITH 4-PRONG *AND* MODULAR
SOCKETS   4.00

P. FLEX
50 FEET, SATIN FINISH, 4 CONDUCTOR CABLING   2.50

Q. SOLID
100 FEET, SOLID CONDUCTORS. 6 IN SHEATH,
COLORED   4.00–5.00

R. SOLID
100 FEET, ROUND PHONE CABLE, 6
CONDUCTOR, BEIGE   7.00

S. INSTALLATION STAPLE GUN   20.00 plus

T. STAPLES
PACKAGES OF 1,000   2.50

U. INSULATED STAPLES
FOR HAMMERING, FASTENING CABLE TO
WALLS, ETC. 50 FOR   1.00

Again, a reminder. The prices shown are single-unit high retail. Almost any telephone installer, TV technician, or student tradesman would probably be able to buy them for 50 or 75 percent of the prices indicated, with further discounts for quantity.

You may feel confused by all this gobbleydegook!

Can you do it? Of course you can.

All you need is a determination to have some fun!

If you can snap a modular telephone jack into its socket, you can certainly do the same with a modular device to control appliances. And you can install the wires and sockets, too! Your telephone provides security, convenience, and pleasure. And best of all, if you decide to have equipment even as fancy as the X-10, it'll be yours, all yours. You will not be paying substantial charges to rent the thing from month to month. Shop for other brands and prices before buying almost everything in telephones.

THE TELEPHONE AND GIGO

The new word "gigo" stands for "Garbage In, Garbage Out"— an alert sounded by computer experts. Their notion is that if you don't put good data into your office or home computer, it won't produce valuable results. The telephone system is of almighty importance to some computer applications. The functions that computers can assist around the home are quite beyond the scope of this book or, indeed, a small set of encyclopedias. There are as many accessories for computers as there are for telephones. The number of programs available to put computers to work is probably infinite.

To list only a few—any computer of merit can readily handle: general ledger accounting, inventory control, accounts payable, mailing lists, time management and control, medical records, household budgeting, and market analysis. If it's an activity of business, the computer can get involved in it.

In games and hobbies, the computer can dish up such things as astrology, quiz games, biorhythms, electronic pinball, mystery puzzles—really, an unending supply of diversions.

The computer can draw illustrations, revise plans, suggest modifications, compare apples and oranges, and generally undertake tasks that would have been utterly beyond human comprehension a few decades ago.

Now you may ask what all this has to do with telephones.

Very simply, telephone connectors and telephone lines give the computer access to banks of data worldwide. And because telephone lines work two ways, your home computer can send its own magic calculations to others, humans and machines, at the speed of light.

INTRODUCING THE MODEM

Until now, when we've talked about telephone connectors and telephone service we've been talking about talking—a very intelligent but relatively slow activity.

111

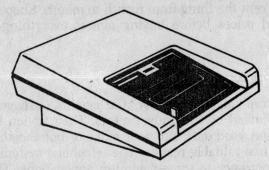

36 / MODEM COUPLER JOINING COMPUTERS TO TELEPHONES

If you and I are talking on the telephone, the frequencies of our voices might be in the range of 300 to 3,000 cycles per second—don't panic, we're not going to get technical. When the computer talks on the telephone it converses in terms of many thousands of cycles. If you don't know what a cycle is, don't let it bother you, you need not know. Besides, this description isn't technically precise. But—just think about the arithmetic involved. Two hundred versus billions!

The computer is millions of times faster at transmitting information than we are but still requires those familiar two wires between your terminal connector and the phone company's central office. And the connecting device will almost certainly be our old friend the modular. Super-computers will require a connector somewhat larger than we've been talking about; it will have eight connectors, perhaps. Sorry, not in this book. We're into home and small business things only.

Between your computer outlet and your telephone socket will sit a gadget called a modem (for modulator, demodulator). It's probably going to look like the gadget in figure 36, a weird little box that sells for $75 to $250 at your friendly computer or electronics store.

Suppose you've computerized a dandy formula for, say, proving Einstein's theories. You want to share it with a friend. But it'll take you at least an hour to read it over the telephone, long-distance, *yikes!*

Follow the action in figure 37.

You pick up your phone and hear the dial tone coming in from your nearby central office, along those two friendly wires.

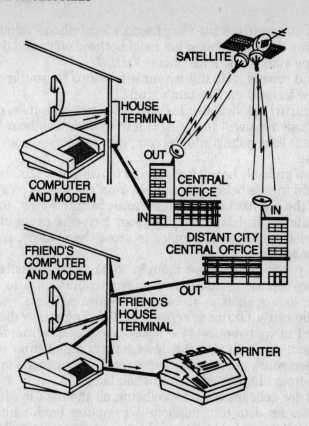

37 / COMPUTER INTERFACING LOCAL OR GLOBAL

You press digit "1," which originates in your set, races past the modular at your phone, out the terminal box on your outside wall, and straight to central office, where the direct-dial computer gets the "1" and registers delight that *your* number is about to go into action, making money for somebody's long-distance network!

You dial your friend's area code, which instantly sets other equipment in motion to enrich the provider, which decides to send your call by way of the satellite, sailing along overhead, 22,300 miles in the stratosphere. The distant city's central office hears its number being called and its circuits are opened, as if by a key.

113

In the next instant your friend's local phone number goes zipping through to his or her neighborhood office and thence on to ring your friend's telephone. "Hello!"

And you say, "Hi, this is your pal. Wanna hit your modem for a new formula on Einstein's stuff?"

Your friend switches his computer to "computer/receive." Or "tape receive." In the next few seconds, the hour-long formula is sent sailing into the computer memory at your friend's house.

You probably have a half minute remaining to talk about family and friends before hanging up. Your call has taken a minute.

If the call has been made at "most favorable rate" times, the minute might have cost you about forty-one cents, though it traveled fifty thousand miles to cross the country, by way of outer space!

If you've never given thought to having a computer in the home, this bit of information may encourage you to take another look at such an accessory for your telephone.

You can subscribe to services available right now that will respond to your requests for ticker-tape displays from the stock market, give you current news reports direct from the news service wires, answer your every request for general or specific data from libraries and information banks.

Major colleges are now collating all the data in all their libraries for data transmission. A computer bank named "The Source" is probably the world's most awesome collection of raw, random, but retrievable data on virtually everything and everybody with impact on earth. Some computer services will arrange to give you, free of charge, limited access to "The Source" or other information banks, when you buy their computers. Depending on the equipment you purchase, the data can be transferred, stored, revised, reviewed, printed out, drawn upon, enhanced, sketched over, and edited repeatedly.

It'll go both ways along those amazing two wires.

If all of that excitement doesn't stir you, think of the possibilities when, say, all the data at Harvard University are swapped with everything at UCLA, collated and checked against each other, item by item. My technical specialist speculates that all of the major research centers of the world which are now taped could pool *all* of their basic data during the course of five or six working days!

Ultra-high-speed data transmission wouldn't be too dependable sent along a couple of flabby old copper wires. Instead, it will travel by way of optical fiber cabling.

Before we leave the subject of computers and data transmission, let's review the optical fiber situation. The tiny cables are being pulled through conduits beneath our streets and highways as these words are written.

So what?

It means that a glasslike cable about the thickness of a pencil can carry thousands of messages back and forth *at higher speeds* and *with greater precision* than anytime before in the history of the planet. The messages are carried by laser beams.

Instead of costly, hard-to-procure copper, the messages are traveling along glasslike material made of the most common matter on earth, little more than everyday sand such as we'd find on the beach—the same old scratchy stuff out of which we make bottles and window panes. Fibers are more satisfactorily connected at junction points. They do everything better than metal wires.

It'll be well into the twenty-first century before fiber technology will totally replace those two all-important metal wires that connect our common, everyday telephones. Just be sure you know the day is coming—fast! Maybe you'll be the first to be switched over to optical fiber. You'll hear an instant improvement in your system.

And it'll all be fastened together by modular plugs and sockets.

You cannot find a more exciting adventure than a visit to your local computer store. For less than a hundred dollars you can enter the computer age. You've actually already done it for much less by simply realizing that the pushbutton pad in your telephone is really the input of a basic computer. You can move forward from that point in any direction you choose.

GUESS WHAT

You've become an expert in the telephone installation game.

More than likely, for openers you've decided to stop paying

monthly rentals for your telephone handsets and have either located some better or cheaper models at department stores, swap meets, and/or your local telephone mart, or made a deal with Ma for the stuff you have now.

From the beginning we said we would tell you all you needed to know about hooking up the two wires that connect your home or business with all of the great big outside world.

That much has been done. There's really nothing more to know.

There are two wires connecting your main phone via a terminal box to your central office. You've run extensions to the locations where you wanted them, testing each of them as you went along. You've added the gadgets that sounded appealing to you. In the process, you've probably made a substantial reduction in your monthly phone bill. If the full benefit of the saving isn't felt immediately, at least you have the satisfaction of knowing the equipment is yours. You'll not be paying, paying, paying, forever, the monthly rental charge that would have been required of you under the old system.

If you bought a $5 swap-meet telephone, its cost will be offset in two or three months. If you went the distance and bought a "decorator fancy," the advantages may not be felt for a bit longer.

With everyday routine care and concern, your telephone equipment should function flawlessly year after year.

The minimum life of the average table-top phone is accepted as roughly twenty years. Our own technical expert, Bud Ball, phoned a half dozen of his acquaintances in Ma Bell companies coast to coast and reported back that in their opinion, residential service calls occur for most householders probably once each decade. And then, the trouble is usually caused by accident rather than casual use.

If something goes wrong, you'll soon figure out whether the fault lies in your wiring, your equipment, or with the phone company. The troubleshooting section of this book begins next.

And if it doesn't exactly make you the world's foremost expert, if you learn to use some of the words correctly, at least you'll sound like you're a pro. I hope you've had fun this far.

PART THREE

Troubleshooting

9 IN CASE YOU EVER HAVE LOCAL PHONE PROBLEMS

There are many activities in which the amateur does better work than the professional. Most dedicated amateur car mechanics drive cars that function better than the comparable models that are hustled in and out of dealer repair shops. Furniture refinishing, dressmaking, and house painting are other routine examples in which keenly motivated amateurs get better results than their production-line counterparts.

If things don't go perfectly the first time, any good amateur will keep at the problem until he or she gets it right. The professional is often required to press ahead to the next job on a tight schedule. Amateurs usually take extra pride in their efforts and results. Professionals will all too often be satisfied if they're not called back by disappointed customers or irate bosses.

So that's why homemade telephone installations are routinely done better than comparable work performed by professionals. We're talking of course about the "entry-level" type of phone installations. Despite care and thoughtfulness, however, glitches can pop up in our routine telephone service.

WE WANT TO AVOID TROUBLES

Whenever you or I decide to install our own phone systems and gadgetry, we do so with the idea of saving money, adding to our pleasure by adding to our facilities, or both.

We start out with the notion that we'll do things right.

First, we want to hook up dependable, fault-free equipment.

119

Second, we want to avoid the annoyance and time-consuming frustrations of troubleshooting. If we install faulty equipment or sloppy wiring or use it all in a haphazard way, chances are we'll be busy correcting our oversights, sooner or later.

There's a third and very important reason to do it carefully. We just happen to have inherited a remarkably good nationwide communications system. The minute we fasten our two wires from residence or office to the terminal or entry box brought to our premises by the phone company, we become part of a global network of elegant facilities which we should respect and maintain.

If we do sloppy work we can expect sloppy service. If that poor work interferes with the system, the phone company will simply disconnect us at their central office if we don't correct our problems. Snip!

Our basic concern of course is always going to be—is the problem on my side of that terminal box or their side?

BEGIN AT THE BEGINNING

There's no scientific basis for the statement but most professionals will agree that most telephone troubles are located *outside* the residential user's location.

Forget for a minute the nerd who regularly leaves his or her telephone off its hook. Skip the sloppy homeowner who can destroy cords as fast as an installer can replace them. In the well-tempered household, telephone service rarely fails. In your own homemade installation there'll be virtually no problems if there's been some tender, loving attention to details as each step is taken.

If you're going to get into the action, start confidently.

The Tools. You'll need a decent screwdriver or two, a pair of pliers, some tape, a pocket knife, hammer and staples or staple gun for cabling.

The Planning. Scratch out a diagram on a pad of paper. No matter how old, your existing house wiring will be usable. You'll be adding to it. Think ahead about equipment you may buy later and plan now how you'll run cabling to plug it in.

The Equipment. During the first years of divestiture, new and used equipment has flooded the market. Make contact with several suppliers and buy from those who are able to give you top quality at the most favorable prices. Look for quality brand names that you can rely on. It won't take you long to discover the good ones.

Test Equipment. With the few gadgets shown in figures 38, 39, and 40, you should be able to work in and out of all known problems. Each of the pieces in figure 38 has a few alligator clips that enable you to fasten readily onto operating circuits or assorted plugs. I asked a TV technician to make up a set such as shown in figure 38 for me to pass along to a relative who expects to go into the telephone installation business when he retires next year. The TV man made up these units from his "junk box" and charged me $6 for all of it.

You'll encounter the word "condensers" and "capacitors" frequently in telephony. They mean the same thing. A condenser is a capacitor and vice versa, for our present purposes.

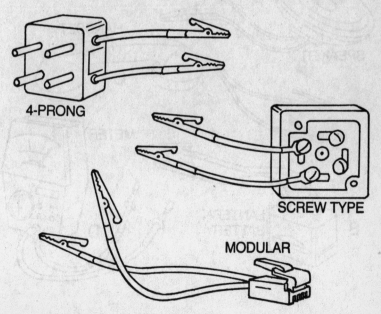

38 / TEST EQUIPMENT PRONG, MODULAR, FOUR-SCREW ADAPTERS

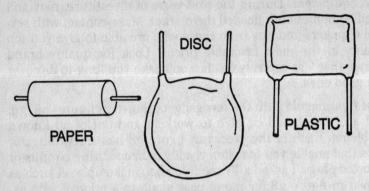

39 / TEST AND SET EQUIPMENT TYPES OF CAPACITORS

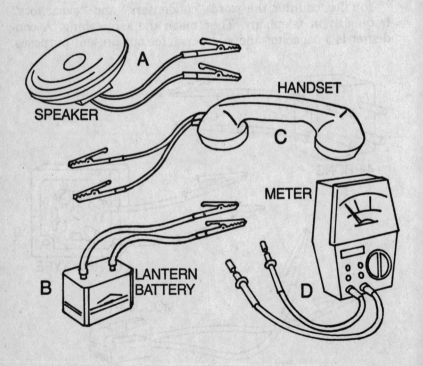

40 / TEST EQUIPMENT SPEAKER, BATTERY, HANDSET, METER

Here are three typical "caps," as they're called by the professionals. Condensers have a capability of stopping the passage of direct current from point to point. But they permit the "pressure" of that voltage to be felt, electronically, from one connector to the other. Sometimes they'll "short" or go "open," almost half the time the reason for failures in ringing systems. Routinely they sell for about twenty-five cents each. If ever in doubt about electricity when testing a circuit, slip a condenser into the alligator clip and probe the circuit with the opposite end. It'll prevent your getting any shock. Naturally, hold on to the insulated, shielded part of the device.

Now, here's a big secret. Look at the four items in figure 40.

At left (A), a discarded radio speaker with a condenser clipped to one lead. Next (B), a simple lantern battery with two foot-long, lightweight wires clipped to its negative and positive terminals.

Next in line (C), an everyday, discarded handset from an old phone. This one has an alligator clip fastened to one wire and a probe to the other. For two or three decades until recently, this instrument was really the principal testing device used by *all* professionals. At right (D), is a volt-ohm microammeter (VOM), selling for about $15. Other than the meter, which is really "professional" equipment, the other items are cheap gadgets which can do virtually *everything* in trouble shooting any telephone system problem. An ordinary flashlight dry cell can be used to test most telephones.

☎ **SPEAKER** CLIPPED ACROSS A LINE IT'LL TELL YOU IF THERE'S A DIAL TONE.

☎ **BATTERY** TOUCHED TO THE ENDS OF THE WIRES FROM A TELEPHONE, THE BATTERY WILL CAUSE A CLICK TO BE HEARD IN THE EARPIECE IF THE SET IS OKAY.

☎ **HANDSET** PROBED INTO A NEW CIRCUIT, IT'LL GIVE YOU THE NICE FAT SOUND OF A DIAL TONE IF THE LINE IS READY FOR USE. CAN BE USED AS AN INTERCOM, SAY, IF YOU'RE ADJUSTING THE DIRECTION OF YOUR TV AERIAL. JUST "TAP" IT ACROSS YOUR HOUSEHOLD PHONE LINES VIA A LONG CORD ON THE ROOF.

☎ **METER** SKIP THE COST AND THE DEVICE UNLESS YOU PLAN TO IMMERSE YOURSELF IN THIS HOBBY OR BUSINESS. THEN, YOU'LL NEED IT TO MEASURE VOLTAGES, CHECK CONTINUITY OF CIRCUITS, LOCATE "OPENS" OR "SHORTS." IT'S GREAT FUN TO HAVE. START OUT WITH THE CHEAPEST NEW MODEL YOU CAN BUY. MAKE SURE YOU GET AN INSTRUCTION SHEET WITH IT (OR CHECK OUT AN INSTRUMENTS BOOK FROM YOUR LIBRARY).

Out of curiosity, I inquired at three different TV repair shops (including one general "fix-it" store) what they'd charge to provide all the items pictured (except the meter) in figures 38, 39, and 40.

The bids from the three technicians for a complete kit were $10, $12.50, and $16.

I was offered two used meters for $10 each.

In other words, if a person wanted to get into the business of home telephone servicing and installation, he or she might be able to do it for about $25 maximum in tools.

For beginners, however, only the flashlight battery is needed, and then only if you're setting out to buy some garage sale equipment, such as basic telephones. Let's go.

THE TELEPHONE

Whether bought new or used, have the instrument tested before leaving the seller's place of business. Unplug a working phone and plug in the item being sold. If it dials a couple of local numbers correctly, you can assume it's okay.

If you are at a swap meet and there's no access to a phone line, simply tap the telephone wires on the leads from the tiny flashlight battery. If you hear vigorous clicks from the phone earpiece, you can assume the instrument is likely to be okay.

ALL OTHER ACCESSORIES

As with telephones, test accessories before leaving the seller's location, whether buying new or used. You may find that some of the adapters pictured in figure 38 will prove handy for these purposes.

On used equipment, you take your own chances without testing.

WIRING

If you've inherited the wiring installed by the phone company in years past, it's all yours to do with as you wish. It's a smart idea to test each link in the service, whether it's old installation or the new wiring you just installed.

FOR APARTMENT DWELLERS IN DISTRESS, ONLY

Occasionally, the apartment dweller will discover that the "hook-up" point for additional phones is in a metal box hanging on the wall in a basement or garage in which there are dozens of incoming wires. And he/she wonders which "pair" belongs to his/her apartment.

If the connection tabs are not clearly coded by letter of apartment or phone number, you can try the following technique. Turn on your stereo and place the phone receiver in front of it. Then hasten to the box, carrying a spare handset with alligator-clip connectors and begin "touching" the probes across adjoining terminals within the box. With luck, you'll stumble quickly upon the pair that belong to you because you'll hear your stereo playing its song or talk. In the process you might stumble over a conversation between another apartment tenant and a third party. In that instant you'll be an illegal phone tapper, so don't listen. Just move on until you find the right "pair." The phone company installers do it all the time, why shouldn't you?

Mark YOUR wire pair clearly and return to your apartment to hang up the phone and continue your installation.

CABLING TEST

1. REMOVE ALL INSTRUMENTS AND ACCESSORIES FROM THE SYSTEM.

2. TOUCH THE LEADS FROM THE BATTERY (ITEM B IN FIGURE 40) QUICKLY, MOMENTARILY, ACROSS THE TWO WIRES OR TERMINALS AT ALL ACCESSIBLE POINTS IN THE SYSTEM. IF YOU SEE A FAINT SPARK,

THERE'S A SHORT CIRCUIT SOMEPLACE. SOMEWHERE ALONG THE PATH OF WIRES, THEY'RE CONTACTING EACH OTHER. ISOLATE AND TRACE THE VARIOUS SPANS OF WIRING UNTIL YOU LOCATE IT.

3. NOW PLUG IN A TELEPHONE AT ANY JACK OR MODULAR SOCKET.

4. ASSEMBLE THE TINY SPEAKER WITH THE BATTERY ACROSS ANY POINT IN THE WIRING, THE CLOSER TO THE TERMINAL BOX THE BETTER. SEE FIGURE 41.

5. IF A GOOD TELEPHONE IS PLUGGED INTO A JACK OR SOCKET, YOU'LL HEAR A CLICK WHEN THE BATTERY CONNECTIONS ARE TOUCHED TO THE WIRE. THE SPEAKER WILL MAKE THE SOUND. EVERYTHING'S IN GOOD SHAPE. TO DOUBLE-CHECK, REMOVE THE TELEPHONE AND REPEAT THE TEST. THIS TIME, WHEN YOU TOUCH THE WIRE TO THE BATTERY, THERE'LL BE NO CLICK AND NO SPARK. YOUR WIRING SHOULD BE READY TO USE. RESTORE THE CONNECTIONS OF ALL THE LEGS OF THE CIRCUIT YOU HAVE DISCONNECTED.

Fasten the two wires of your internal phone system to the two connections in the terminal box brought up to your house and wired in place by the phone company.

Plug in your telephone. Hear a dial tone?

Splendid. Phone a friend and say, "You'll never guess what I just did."

If you've traveled deluxe and purchased a meter, as seen in figure 39, you can readily test instruments by removing them from any circuit and placing the meter on the 1,000 ohm (1K) scale. Touch the test probes to the telephone wire ends and then make puffing sounds into the telephone mouthpiece. Your wheezes should send the meter needle zapping up and down.

Inside the handset is the magnetic-dynamic earphone which reproduces sounds by the motion of its diaphragm back and forth according to the electrical impulses that reach its nearby magnetic coils. The transmitter, or mouthpiece, is a tiny metal box full of carbon dust. The lid of the box is also a flexible diaphragm cover that moves back and forth with the pressures of the speaker's voice. The carbon dust in the box is thus compressed and relaxed, sent convulsing into frantic configurations that change the resistance values between the poles (conductors) fastened to the box. Unscrew the mouthpiece on a handset. The transmitter will probably fall out into your hand. It'll add to your know-how about telephones.

MOST OFTEN ENCOUNTERED TROUBLES

IMPORTANT NOTE: In the new system of phone service, you can be cheerfully honest about everything relating to your phone service. The repair operator will appreciate knowing what you've done, and your information will speed up the location of the problem in the central office or in the lines between the central and your location.

NO DIAL TONE

You can't call out. Also, you can't be reached. Is the fault in your equipment or in Ma's?

1. TRY EACH PHONE IN YOUR SYSTEM. MAYBE ONLY ONE IS A "NO-TONE."

2. NO? THEN UNPLUG EACH ACCESSORY AND LISTEN TO HEAR IF A DIAL TONE RETURNS IN THE REMAINING SETS OR YOUR TEST SET.

3. NO? THEN, TO DETERMINE IF THE PROBLEM IS A SHORT OR OPEN IN *YOUR* WIRING OR THE PHONE COMPANY'S, "LIFT" (DISCONNECT) THE WIRES WHERE YOU ATTACHED THEM TO THE ENTRY TERMINAL BOX. CLIP YOUR TEST HANDSET (WITH THE ALLIGATOR CLIPS) ACROSS THE PHONE COMPANY'S WIRES. DIAL TONE? IF YES, THE PROBLEM *MUST* BE IN YOUR INSTALLATION. IF NO DIAL TONE AT THIS JUNCTION, PHONE THE REPAIR SERVICE OFFICE AND ASK THEM TO LOCATE THE PROBLEM IN THEIR LINES FROM CENTRAL OFFICE.

4. IF YOU DID HAVE A DIAL TONE AT THE ENTRY TERMINAL, YOU'LL HAVE TO CHECK THE WIRING AT EACH TERMINAL IN THE SYSTEM. THE OPEN OR SHORT IS FIRST ASSUMED TO EXIST BETWEEN THE ENTRY TERMINAL AND YOUR *FIRST* PHONE CONNECTOR.

5. IF THE DIAL TONE CAN BE HEARD AT THE FIRST TERMINAL THEN PROCEED ALONG TO YOUR OTHER EXTENSION TERMINALS, ISOLATING EACH UNTIL THE FAULTY WIRING OR SOCKET CONNECTION IS FOUND.

MORE TROUBLE——YOU'RE TOLD YOU CAN'T BE CALLED

Friends, relatives, or neighbors tell you in person that your line must be out of order. Maybe they've been getting the routine "out of service" recorded message, or hours of busy signals.

Before inviting the repair service out for a costly service call, follow the procedure outlines for no dial tone. It can save you bagfuls of money.

1–REMOVE PHONE
2–INSERT HANDSET OR RADIO SPEAKER
3–LISTEN FOR DIAL TONE

OR

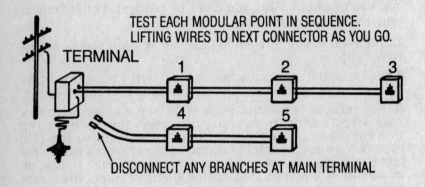

TEST EACH MODULAR POINT IN SEQUENCE.
LIFTING WIRES TO NEXT CONNECTOR AS YOU GO.

TERMINAL

DISCONNECT ANY BRANCHES AT MAIN TERMINAL

OR

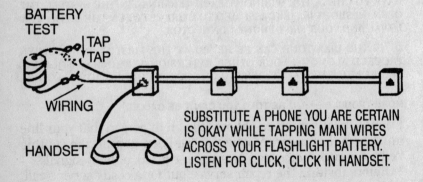

BATTERY
TEST

TAP
TAP

WIRING

HANDSET

SUBSTITUTE A PHONE YOU ARE CERTAIN
IS OKAY WHILE TAPPING MAIN WIRES
ACROSS YOUR FLASHLIGHT BATTERY.
LISTEN FOR CLICK, CLICK IN HANDSET.

41 / TEST ASSEMBLY ANOTHER WAY TO TROUBLESHOOT

CALLS ARE FULL OF STATIC, NOISE, AND CRACKLING

If the condition persists beyond a few hours, simply disconnect the wires at the terminal box, clip in a substitute telephone and make a call. If it's still noisy, the problem belongs to the phone company. It's their task to fix the line to central without charge.

But if the call is now clear, start looking in your own system for loose connections, frayed wires, wobbly plugs, or tired instruments. Clean the hook switch contacts inside the instrument. Simply drag a strip of bond paper between the contacts.

As usual, the best way to check telephone instruments is by *substitution*. Plug your equipment into a neighbor's modular socket and see if it works well there.

Or borrow a neighbor's good telephone and connect it throughout your system. The resulting sounds should lead you quickly to the trouble area. The socket that causes the racket may have a loose, corroded, or shorting wire connection.

BASE CORD TROUBLES

Frayed and tired wires will cause noisy, static-crackly calls.

Twist the instrument's wires along their lengths to the connector on the wall.

When you come to any section where the internal conductors are creating problems, you'll know it. If the crackling doesn't get worse, the set will probably simply go dead.

Before discarding the whole cord, try attaching a different wire or wires within the sheath.

Replacement wires from any terminal to the base of phone or handset are relatively cheap. But when you open the base of the phone, take your time—replace the connecting wires one by one, maintaining the color coding.

RINGER TROUBLES

If you determine that one of your telephones is a-okay except it refuses to ring, locate the ringing capacitor (see Part Four, figure 42). It's usually the culprit. A replacement capacitor can be bought for twenty-five cents. Or maybe easier—sometimes the ringing circuit has simply been disconnected or turned to "off." Check the lever or thumb switch in the base of the phone.

DIALS AND PADS

Contrary to some expert opinion, telephone rotary dials can often go sour, always making the same mistake, maybe connecting you with the same wrong number every time you dial. It'll hardly be worth repairing because surely, by this time it'll have made millions upon millions of switching pulses. Save the telephone for spare parts, but remove it from service. The handset should make a dandy test monitor.

If yours doesn't give you sufficient volume, open the earpiece and see if there's a small varistor (transistor), a thing that looks like a large bead, soldered across the wiring. Snip one end of the little thing. The amplified sound should jump sky-high!

Pushbutton phones will occasionally go on the rampage. The reason? Each number on the tone pad generates two frequencies or tone sounds when it's depressed. Sometimes, though rarely, one of the frequencies will simply quit. You can still hear a sound when you press the buttons, but it'll take an expert to detect the absence of a single tone. There are basically only seven frequencies in the tone system. Each digit combines a different pair of them.

If a pushbutton phone consistently gives you wrong numbers (the same or variable numbers) and fails in a substitution test, take it out of service, using it selectively for spare parts.

BELL TAP

If your system includes all rotary dial phones or a mixture of dials and pushbuttons, sometimes the "bell" will tap on an extension when another phone is being dialed. Most of the time the annoyance can be corrected by reversing the base phone connections on the "tapper" (the hammer that strikes the bell in response to pulses of electricity). If not, adjust the spring tension on the tapper.

☎ SUMMARY

The chapter has surely covered more than 95 percent of the problems that beset most telephones, residential systems, and central offices. Consider right now that you probably have enough equipment and know-how to avoid forever even one expensive service call from any phone company. And that's a fact!

PART FOUR

An Inside Look at Things Present and Future

10 LONG-DISTANCE ALTERNATIVES

You might offset some of the monstrous increases in local dial tone costs by switching into a long-distance service that is *not* owned and operated by Ma Bell.

Let's get right to the point. *If you spend less than $250 a year for long distance, on average less than $20 a month, SKIP THIS CHAPTER.* Stick with the local and Ma Bell (AT&T) system you now have and close your eyes to all the attractive ads. If you're spending more than $20 montly just for long distance, *Kiss Ma Bell Good-bye* and consider a different service. You will have to do your own choosing. Each locality and individual has different needs and services. You must get the system that suits you and your pocketbook best. The service must be operational in your community. It must be able to reach the distant points you contact most often. Only *you* know about those things. Use this chapter only as a guide to help you get the most long-distance quality for your money.

YOUR BILL TELLS THE STORY

Until divestiture, when Ma Bell was required to reorganize her twenty-three local companies, most telephone bills were a form of fiction. Charges were "bundled," which is to say, your "dial tone" charge was lumped in with the rental charge for your main instrument and each extension. If there were long-distance charges, they'd be listed separately. The money you sent to the phone company would trickle *upward* to Ma Bell's headquarters, and a little bit would trickle back to pay for the heat and light bills and staff salaries at the local level. It would be unfair not to repeat that Ma Bell would use lots of her long-distance revenues to subsidize local company services.

Nowadays, when you look at your bill you see all the horrors laid out for inspection—"unbundled." Prices shown are estimates from around the continent's phone companies. I'm guessing, but they should cover about nine out of ten telephone customers. A few years ago I heard from a stranger who was paying $225 a month for a line to his mountain cabin, for example. That's unusual. These are for "average" folks.

LOCAL ACCESS (the two wires which bring you your dial tone, from the central office) $5–$30 per line

LONG-DISTANCE ACCESS. Beginning 1985, every residence was charged $2 monthly, EXTRA, because the local lines would also connect to long-distance services. Ma Bell gets most of that extra loot because she invented the service. Your other long-distance supplier, if you use one, will not share in that windfall; your local company keeps what Ma Bell doesn't.

EXTRA CHARGE FOR "TONE" SERVICE	$0–$3 monthly
EQUIPMENT RENTAL—typically,	
STANDARD DESK SET, ROTARY	$1–$3 monthly
STANDARD DESK SET, TONE	$2–$5 monthly
WALL OR COMPACT, ROTARY	$2.50–$6.50 monthly
WALL OR COMPACT, TONE	$3.50–$7.50 monthly
SPEAKERPHONE, ROTARY OR TONE	$10–$15 monthly
NEW HOOK-UP (*first time*)	$20–$200 per line
VISIT FOR REPAIR (*rental equipment*)	$0–$100 a visit
VISIT FOR REPAIR (*customer-owned*)	$35 and up, *no limit!*
REPAIRS EXTERIOR *to your premises*	$0 (in most cases)
NONLOCAL "TOLL AREA" *add-ons*	5–50 cents per minute
INFORMATION CALLS	0–25 cents a call

134

LONG-DISTANCE SERVICE

(YOU WILL SEE LISTED HERE THE NAME OF THE COMPANY YOU'RE USING AND THE TOTAL OF THE DETAIL IN YOUR CALLS)

SURCHARGES	(VARIES WITH AREA——SEE GTE STORY, P. 136)
TAXES, FEDERAL, STATE, AND LOCAL	1%–5% each
SPECIAL FEES (HANDICAPPED, ETC.)	1% of base rate
EXTRA CHARGE FOR BUSINESS LINE	$20–$50 monthly
LATE CHARGES	1.5%–2%
BOUNCED-CHECK CHARGE-ONS	$10–$25
VERIFYING OR INTERRUPT CHARGES	Average $1
NONLISTING OF YOUR NUMBER*	50 cents– $1 monthly
ADDITIONAL LISTING IN WHITE PAGES	50 cents –$1 monthly
ADVERTISING IN YELLOW PAGES	

(VARIES WIDELY, AREA TO AREA, WITH SIZE OF MARKET. BUT A QUARTER-PAGE AD IN A MAJOR MARKET COULD READILY COST $2,000–$3,000 PER MONTH. NOW THEY MAKE UP "CONSUMER" AND "BUSINESS" BOOKS SEPARATELY FOR INCREASED REVENUES).

* Eliminate this charge by listing a fictitious name.

If you don't examine your phone bill each month, line by line, you're certain to be a loser. The "new" phone companies, the Seven Sisters that developed out of Ma Bell's conglomerate, as well as the few super-independents, such as General Telephone and, in Canada, the Canada Bell System have been punching up their basic rates nonstop.

In my own telephone area, serviced by General Telephone, rates jumped 21.3 percent in 1984, with pleadings under way for much bigger increases in '86. Pacific Telephone is assured an increase of more than a billion dollars in 1986. The Pacific customers may finally say, "Hell, no!" Ameritech, serving the central Midwest area around Chicago, will be going for a billion-dollar gulp after getting several giant swallows of increase. The companies seem to think little or nothing of going to the public utilities commissions (PUCs) and asking for gigantic rate hikes, undoubtedly on the premise that they'll have to settle for less than their request. It gives the PUC a chance to say, "See, people! We held prices down." And the phone company's top managers invariably wail that they'll barely scrape up next week's payroll, then give their top managers substantial raises. And while waiting lists for technical services grow even longer, they'll hire more lawyers and fire more technicians. That's the pattern in most big businesses today, not only utility companies.

Again, the little family group is bearing the burden. Big companies, the multiconglomerates, with unprecedented profits for most of them in recent years, are saying, "What? Another phone bill increase? To hell with them."

And they set up their own internal system, usually with ingenious links into the national/ international phone networks—all at immense savings. The charges are shoved over on to the backs of residential users and Social Security pensioners, who look at their incoming phone bills and feel nauseous! Are we unorganized, passive, dumb—or all three?

Meanwhile, the local electric companies are rocket-boosting their rates to pay off the overcharges and mistakes within their Mad Hatter nuclear generators! If this were not an era that blessed the super-rich and damned the peasantry and superpoor, the shareholders would be required to pay. Sooner or later, "we, the people" will wake up and demand some fair play from the super-conglomerates and public utilities that *we* created in the first place. It's vital for every ratepayer, even the shareholders in utilities, to join a local consumer group—see page 157!

CASE IN POINT

One customer among the millions served mostly on the West Coast and western Canada by General Telephone ("my" phone company) caught the company picking our pockets. Carl

136

Kriensky of Santa Monica saw a possible overcharge in his bill. (Though I'd checked my own, I missed it.) General, or GTE, as we know it, like all phone companies, bills (and receives) for basic charges a month in advance. Carl had paid his August 17 bill, the basic rate and long-distance and tolls and taxes, along with the temporary 21.3 percent surcharge tentatively okayed by the public utilities commission. But Carl's basic service charge had already been increased by 21.3 percent over the previous month (after PUC's final okay)—hence he was being billed *twice* for the increase. He asked the company, "How come?" and received a lot of aggravation, according to his own description. Eventually, his persistence paid off. GTE admitted their accounting people had been "working on it," uncertain as to how the rate increase was already in the bills, according to the company's spokesperson.

By October, GTE's spectacular computers and money wizards came clean. They'd screwed up again! As a result of Carl Kriensky's scanning of his bill, GTE had to return the $5.1 million it pocketed illegally from its 2.4 million customers in California. My own share of the refund was almost $3, credited to my November bill. Moral: Don't trust utility companies, health service providers, conglomerates, or gold brick salesmen, or _____ (add your own in this space).

But we met here today to talk about cutting your gigantic phone bill. The best and easiest place to start is installing and maintaining your own equipment, *yourself*. The next best bet to bop Ma Bell is to stop using her overpriced long-distance service, if your monthly cost exceeds $20.

400 ALTERNATIVES

One of my best friends at one of the "new" phone companies estimates that there are about a thousand-plus "resellers" of long-distance service, but he knows for a fact there are more than 400 out there, right now, setting up shop. The shake-out in reselling long distance will prove to be titanic as companies compete each other to shreds.

We start with Ma Bell's long-distance system, in most locations obtained by dialing "1" followed by the area code and local number. There are a half dozen other "common carriers" like AT&T long-distance. They include MCI, Sprint, SBS, ARGO, Western Union, and a few others that have their own transmission equipment, microwaves, satellites, and wiring. Routinely, they're referred to as OCCs (Other Common Carriers). The hundreds of others, including Allnet, U.S. Telephone, Telesaver, and TDX, buy their service at discount rates from Ma Bell or the OCCs. As my friend says, there are definitely 400 of them.

Their licenses to do business vary. There are some that are limited to long calls within a state and others that can provide service at the so-called LATA level—Local Access and Transport Area. The FCC has divided the continental USA into 162 such areas, which are allegedly bounded by commercial, topographical, or other considerations. Most are confined within state lines. At least there is a measure of control as well as healthy competition—healthy for the winners, in any event.

WHAT'S THE BEST DEAL?

In the earlier edition of *Kiss Ma Bell Good-bye* I was able to compare the charges among five of them; Skyline still was gearing up. I used AT&T's familiar old schedule of different prices for different times of the day. You can't make such comparisons anymore. The new resellers are creating new ways to attract customers, basing their charges on "seconds in use," "miles covered," "6-second intervals," "lower membership rates," even "NO use, NO pay."

Take Ma Bell's "old system" of charging for starters.

She makes her big money between 8:00 A.M. and 5:00 P.M. on weekdays. Full rate. A call from Los Angeles to New York, direct dial, no operator involved, will cost 69 cents for first minute, plus 46 cents for each additional minute. Weekends, the same calls will cost you 60 percent less. (By the way, the 60 percent discount applies straight through from 11:00 P.M. Friday to 5:00 P.M. Sunday, and across the board seven days a week between 11:00 P.M. and 8:00 A.M.). Daily, from 5:00 P.M. until 11:00 P.M. you will get only a 40 percent discount. But wait a minute, you poor, mind-boggled telephoner! With AT&T you don't have to sign new papers or do anything more than you've done for years. Dial "1" (most places), then your area code and desired seven-digit number!

THAT'S NICE, BUT . . .

Until 1985, Ma Bell's long-distance rates were usually a lot higher than the prices charged by the other companies. Some of the others actually buy their services at a discount from Ma and sell them to you cheaper than Ma Bell would charge through the local company you're now hooked up with. I can buy long-distance services through American Express, a few department stores, and lots of other bank credit cards that might make a few pennies on each of my calls. Their charges will appear on my monthly statement. Or you and I can buy direct.

Of course, unless you're located in the "equal access" zones like parts of Virginia, you'll be busy dialing numbers—as many as twenty-three plus, if you go from Ma Bell's shop to the Polka Dot long-distance group (or whatever). It'll be a while before we all get equal access. Veterans at Bell have been predicting the mid-1990s. Bud Ball, my technical double-checker, says we could have equal access, continentally, within two years! It depends on the government agencies and elected politicians!

There are, as of publication time, twenty different ways of buying into the six *largest* long-distance firms. Each service company is different from the others.

It nearly blew my mini-computer's lid, but I was able to compare the "top eight" very loosely on the basis of a 4-minute-18-second call about 8:00 P.M. any weeknight.

L.A. TO	AT&T	SPRINT	MCI	SKYLINE	ITT	W.UNION	ALLNET	TELESAVE
Chicago	$1.44	1.29	1.13	1.00	1.30	1.10	.90	1.08
Miami	2.70	2.10	2.18	1.90	2.40	2.44	1.80	2.49 (N/A)
New York	2.70	2.46	2.16	2.40	2.55	2.70	1.80	2.25

N/A – Service Not Available at time of calculation

Involved in the calculations were mileage, satellite and microwave availabilities, and the supposition that there'd be no initial fees or start-up charges.

139

OTHER CONSIDERATIONS

A glance at the chart above would suggest that Allnet was the most consistent low-cost service. But Allnet wants a $7.50 initiation fee plus $5 a month even if you don't make a single long-distance call. Skyline in Los Angeles gets a $16 start-up fee and $15 monthly minimum. Skyline (owned jointly by IBM, the typewriter/computer/you-name-it giant of giants; Comsat, the satellite company; and Aetna, the insurance company), then proved to me (using their figures) that if my long-distance tolls last year were really within pennies of a thousand dollars, they would have given me exactly the same locations and time of calls for $575—almost half of Ma Bell's charges! By their computers, too, they estimated that MCI would have charged me more than $800. Nevertheless, forsooth, and notwithstanding . . .

I'd just about decided to go with MCI, in large part because of my excessive calling back and forth into Canada, where books like this are sold and, hence, researched. MCI Telecommunications threw its own satellites up into the stratosphere, where they stay in stationary orbit 22,300 miles overhead. They could give me cheaper calls into Canada, for which Ma Bell charges eye-fuzzing prices. Furthermore, MCI had been at the game longer, had, in fact, *founded* the alternate service after fighting Ma Bell's courtroom lawyers for years and *really* winning a big one. MCI had already nipped off almost 2 million of Ma's 86 million long-distance callers. More than 400 of the Fortune 500 companies use bits, pieces, or all of MCI services. Using *my* figures *they* proved I'd save between 5 and 40 percent on all my regular long-distance calls. Wow! They had overnight mail (though at a whopping cost), even an MCI WATS system (of which more later). And the price was better than AT&T's. And they all but said their quality of service, their fidelity of tone, was better than Ma Bell's. Oh? That did it! Tomorrow I'd sign up, or phone up, or cheer up, blow up—or something!

Next morning the paper arrived, headlining news that MCI's basic rate structure would have to be increased "an average 5%!" I postponed my decision and sobbed something about using the mails more often. From across the breakfast table I heard a familiar voice remind me that the cost of postage was headed up, too! I gave up! In March 1985, Postal rates jumped 10 percent first class, even more for other services!

ONE DAY'S DALLYING

That same day, I dialed personally every long-distance service among the big eight. I heard prices by the minute, the mile, and the time of day. I spent a couple of hours on "hold" waiting for the "next available consultant" to get off the horn and talk to me. Two of the biggest companies didn't have any information of the type I wanted. One didn't even answer its own telephones for new subscribers. Maybe they hadn't paid their own bills!

ARE YOU READY FOR THIS?

You pay an extra $2 a month on your phone bill just because the two wires to your central office have the built-in capability of conveying long-distance calls to *any* system. It applies to your bill even if you have never made a long-distance call and never plan to do so. After all, somebody might call *you* long distance, eh? You'll be stuck an extra $24 a year. Many small resellers are going *plop*—"Sorry, those lines have been disconnected, the deadbeats!"—because the subsidy won't make their services so attractive.

BIG AND GROWING BIGGER

Another of the real big hunks is Sprint, started on bailing wire and now a multimillion-dollar baby of the General Telephone Company. That acquisition was enough to scare me off Sprint, though only briefly. I'd complained bitterly about General's service in the first edition of this book, probably unfairly.

General Tel's service has been getting better, day by day. They've installed some new switches and data transmission services that set new standards. Unfortunately, they tend to hang on to their fifty-year-old junk and use it in other areas that have more patient customers than "Hey man, let's get with it, eh?" Californians. But Sprint's prices, quality of signal, genuine effort, and now a trio of new satellites launched by Arianespace, the private rocket launchers, in France, convince me they're great.

If you live near Indianapolis, your mobile phone service will be set up by GTE's Mobilnet. These fellows don't let any grass grow under their feet. In recent times, even Standard and Poor's, the corporation that rates all companies for shareholder reliability, upgraded the company from A-2 to A-1 in commercial paper and from triple B to A in preferred stock. Not bad. If they keep up the good work, I'll find myself praising them ecstatically.

ADDING UP APPLES AND ORANGES

The amazing reporters and researchers of *U.S. News & World Report* have been kind to me, as usual, in tabulating the current standings (runnings?) in the long-distance marathon.

WHO'S WHO IN LONG DISTANCE

FIRM NAME	REVENUE (APPROX)	MARKETS SERVED	CUSTOMERS
AT&T	$35 billion	All of them	86 million
MCI	$1.5–$2 billion	375	1.5–2.0 million
Sprint	$800 million +	353	900,000+
Allnet	$180–200 million	180–200	150,000–175,000
ITT	$165 million +	113+	125,000
Western Union	$60 million +	135+	110,000
U.S. Telephone	$135 million	67	90,000
Skyline	Not Available	41	90,000

Note that Telesave is not listed, probably overtaken by U.S. Telephone in this type of comparison.

The foregoing chart was developed by Sanford Bernstein & Company for *USN&WR*—to which the author is deeply indebted—also for another subscription renewal. There it is. AT&T gets about 77 percent of all long-distance business. Local companies, those spun off from Bell, are picking up about 17 percent, mostly from long distance within their coverage area—it's allowed. The remaining 6 percent is divided among the seven other biggies in the chart and about 400 Mom and

Pop and small strivers, all aching to be profitable resellers, fast going broke.

WHO'S GOT THE BEST SERVICE?

A nonprofit organization called Consumers Checkbook, financed by Consumers Union and a Committee for Lower Phone Costs, did an immense survey of long-distance customers.

They interviewed hundreds, nay, thousands of "alternative" buyers. In terms of pure quality, the winners, #1 through #8 turned out to be:

SKYLINE	TELESAVER
AT&T	MCI
GTE SPRINT	ITT
ALLNET	WESTERN UNION

I shall subscribe to Skyline—no, Sprint—ah, t'heck with it. I'll call them all again tomorrow. So, must you, if you're looking to save money.

THE ULTIMATE DECISION

You must do your own research. You must check out the systems available *in your community*. Get a price list from them, city to city, and try to compare each with all the others. Find out if they have an initiation fee and monthly charge. If yes, how much and how is it credited against calls you make?

If you're fanatic about long-distance service (and it might be worth it), get the best information available, hopefully kept up to date in a pamphlet-type book entitled "The Complete Guide to Lower Phone Costs." Send $6.95, which includes the postage, to Lower Phone Costs, 806 15th Street NW, Suite 925, Washington, DC 20005.

SELECTING YOUR OWN SYSTEM

So you make up your mind to *Kiss Ma Bell Good-bye* and set out to see what else is available in the telephone supermarkets. How do you plan to make the best choice?

The best place to start is one of your average phone bills, the one where you ran up more than $20 worth of long distance for the fifth or sixth month in a row—okay? Use a chart like the one below, or draw your own version and start working, just as I did, calling the available OCCs and resellers.

All the OCCs have free 800 numbers. I'd list them here for you, but the numbers vary from place to place. Dial 1-800-555-1212 and ask for the toll-free numbers of two or three of the names you've heard in your area—Sprint, MCI, Skyline, ITT, Western Union—or others. Incidentally, you can buy your own "800" telephone directory. Phone them at 1-800-242-4634.

For the resellers serving your area with intrastate or interstate service, there's no harm in asking your local telephone business office for help. No matter who you choose, your local office is going to get a chunk of revenue for "accessing" your wires to theirs. Got it?

Almost certainly, the service operator you call will ask your own area code and the prefix (first three numbers) of your present phone. He or she will then ask how you can be helped. You say you'd like to compare *their* charges with the rates you paid for, say, three long-distance calls via your present carrier, probably AT&T. You *must* be prepared now to tell the service advisor (a) the area code and prefixes you called, (b) the time of day or night, (c) whether it was direct-dial or operator-assisted, and (d) the length of your call. All of this information will be listed on your own, personal bill.

Also, you should be prepared to tell the operator the *distance in miles, as the crow flies,* between *your* location and your destination calls. You'll need a map, perhaps. Round off your mileage to the nearest fifty miles, if you can.

MY OWN AREA CODE IS _____, MY TELEPHONE PREFIX IS _____.

CALL TO AREA AND PREFIXES (DISTANCE)	LENGTH OF CALL AND TIME, TYPE	AT&T CHARGED ME	WOULD CHARGE	WOULD CHARGE	WOULD CHARGE
TOTALS--------------------		$ _____	$ _____	$ _____	$ _____

Make as many comparisons in the right-hand columns as you desire. You may want to call all the options. You may settle for two or three.

AT THIS POINT YOUR ASSESSMENT IS HALF COMPLETED. THERE ARE SOME OTHER VITAL THINGS YOU MUST LEARN ABOUT YOUR "ALTERNATE SYSTEM." Have a chart, like the one shown below, standing by, ready. Go down the questions, one by one, with your customer advisor on the other end of the line.

QUESTIONS	SAID	SAID	SAID
1. Do you charge a monthly minimum?	___	___	___
2. Is there a monthly fee?	___	___	___
3. Is there an initial "start-up" fee?	___	___	___
4. Can I reach anywhere in the country?	___	___	___
5. Do your rates vary with distance?	___	___	___
6. Do your rates vary by time of day?	___	___	___
7. Do you have "equal access" yet?	___	___	___
8. Do I pay more for my first minute?	___	___	___
9. Do you "round off" time charges?	___	___	___
10. What makes *your* service best?	___	___	___
11. Credit for wrong numbers?	___	___	___
12. Operator assistance available?	___	___	___
13. _____	___	___	___
14. _____	___	___	___

Add in any questions that still bother *you* in lines 13 and 14.

You'll have the answers staring back at you. Before thanking the consumer advisor and signing off, ask the person to mail you any data or sign-up applications you will need. You may want to ask if they'll have a "charge-card" available for when you're away from home.

If you still need more information before settling on an optional long-distance service, write for the "Lower Phone Costs" book I suggested to you on page 143. Make sure, when you write (with your check for $6.95 enclosed) that you'll be receiving an up-to-date edition, or skip it!

. . . AND IN CONCLUSION . . .

The parts of the "Lower Phone Costs" book I enjoyed most proved that it pays to buy, not rent, telephone equipment and then proceeded to list the best places to buy such equipment—in their opinion, first, second, and third: catalogue company showrooms, discount appliance stores, and discount department stores. No points for the local phone company store, if you notice! (I'm not so sure. I recently bought an auto-dialer at my local phone mart, cheaper than discount.)

And it concluded that section by commenting, "Except in a few exceptional circumstances, you save by buying. Someday, in fact, renting a phone will probably seem about as silly as renting a toaster or blender."

Now—y'see? What have I been saying to you from the very beginning.

11 THINGS YOU MAY NOT HAVE KNOWN ABOUT PHONES, BUT WERE AFRAID TO ASK

Figure 42 reveals the inner parts of a standard telephone.

All instruments are essentially the same on the inside. Snoopy has the same innards as Mickey Mouse now that they've both become popular figures.

Different manufacturers use different types of base plates. The numbers that are imprinted on these plates vary from unit to unit. In one telephone, if you open up the case, you might find a red conductor clipped on to a terminal numbered 14. On the next phone, the same terminal might bear the number 45. The words of caution are provided here for the individual who, say, is changing the base cord. Remove old wires and snap on new ones artfully. One wire at a time, please.

There are springs that lift the hook switch when the receiver is lifted. Other springs control the tensions on the tapper. The other hardware includes diodes, straps, coils, and assorted switches that are just about the same in all phones made during the past half century.

We can get an idea of how calls are completed, in and out of your residence.

INCOMING CALLS

When the central office receives a call for you, the electro-mechanical or digital switches close on the two wires leading

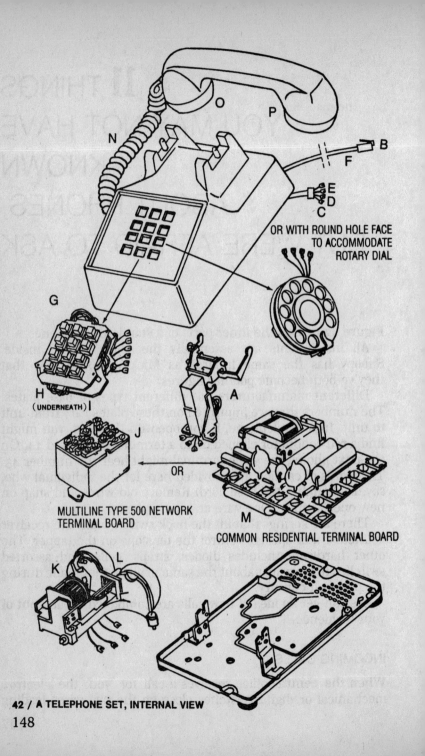

OR WITH ROUND HOLE FACE
TO ACCOMMODATE
ROTARY DIAL

(UNDERNEATH)

MULTILINE TYPE 500 NETWORK
TERMINAL BOARD

COMMON RESIDENTIAL TERMINAL BOARD

42 / A TELEPHONE SET, INTERNAL VIEW

148

to your residence. A blip of alternating current is shot down the line, past your terminal and into your incoming cord (F). It zips past the modular connector (B) and scoots through that section of the hook switch (A) which is being held in correct position by the weight of the handset. Depending on your system, the current will be fluctuating at a rate of twenty-five cycles per second (there are a dozen frequencies in general use). Party-line telephones share a single pair of wires back to the central office. But the telephone ringer in each household along the line is assigned a different frequency, like twenty-five cycles per second, thirty, forty, etc., and the phone companies' engineers work it all out in advance of hook-up. Otherwise, party-line users would go bell-happy. Even if there are five homes on a single line, only the telephone home being called will have its bell ringing. Party line or single residence, the procedure's about the same, thanks to differing ringer frequencies. The central office equipment sends one-second pulses with four-second pauses in between. The current is enough to scramble through the wiring, usually taking the routes through red (C) and yellow (E). Often the yellow wire and green wire (D) will be plugged in to the same terminal. The pulse of electricity slams into the condenser (M), which blocks the direct current component on the line and allows the alternating current to reach the finger coil. In this way, the ringer coil (K) is magnetized on and off to attract and repel the bell tapper (L) from side to side, to ring your bell. The loudness of the bell is often controlled by the amount of tension on the spring, which is adjustable by a lever or wheel peeking out through the base of the phone. Remember, during all of this time, there's another voltage (direct current) already squatting on that same pair of lines, just itching to get into action. The power is supplied from a monstrous storage battery at central. The battery is a mammoth version of the one that starts your car.

A HOOK SWITCH. B INCOMING MODULAR. C RING CONNECTOR (USUALLY RED). D TIP CONNECTOR (USUALLY GREEN). E GROUND LEAD (USUALLY YELLOW). F INCOMING CORD. G PUSHBUTTON PAD. H CRYSTAL CONTROLLER. I TONE GENERATOR. J INDUCTION COIL. K BELL AND RINGER COIL. L BELL TAPPER. M RINGER CONDENSER. N HANDSET CORD. O TRANSMITTER. P EARPIECE (RECEIVER).

Well, you hear the bell, which usually rings just when you get in the shower or bath. You dash to the telephone and lift the receiver, stretching the handset cord (N). But before that cord has even wiggled, the weight removal causes the hook switch (A) to flip to its other correct position. The ringing voltage is immediately cut off back at central. Only the direct current remains "on line."

You say "Hello" into the transmitter (O) of the handset and the sound is transposed from air motion to electrical activity in the transmitter back along the wires to your own phone and that of your caller. Zap, zing, whish!

As you start talking, the tiny, dustlike granules of carbon within the transmitter are blapped around between the incoming and outgoing connectors, one of which is connected to a flexible diaphragm or "lid on the box."

WHILE YOU'RE TALKING, THINGS ARE HAPPENING

Each inflection, breath, word, causes the carbon granules to compress and relax in accordance with the in-and-out movements of the diaphragm on the little carbon containers. As the carbon dust slams every which way within the boxes, the resistance to electricity is changing. Thus, the amount and shape of audio frequency voltage is being changed as it scrams back and forth along the direct current path that now exists on the wires between your phone and that of your caller. And those frequencies are of an alternating type which is simultaneously slipping through the primary windings of the tiny induction coil (J). There are two voltages now present in that coil and they get together to flow out along the wires. The coil is simply a minispool of two ultrafine wires. The fluctuations of voltage on the inner spool (primary) cause changes on the wiring wrapped around it (secondary) and a smidgeon of that current is called the side-tone, which is fed back into the earpiece and is a tiny "dynamic" listening device.

The foregoing description will drive most telephone engineers into a state of hysteria because they'd use much longer words. If you'd like to learn those words, the best place to apply is your local community college, most of which conduct regular and extension courses in telephony. I hope by now you've begun to realize that telephone things are every bit as interesting and important as other utilities and facilities in our lives.

Meanwhile, at the central office, if your call is on a toll or long-distance basis, a mini-section of the revenue computer is counting off the seconds as you yak-yak-yak, standing there fresh from the shower. If you have a hunch the central office locations are maintained under tight security, you can believe that the computers that measure the billing time of your basic service and toll calls are maintained tighter than Fort Knox. There are so many interlocks, security-fixes, electronic, manual, and human guards hovering over the *revenue computers* that nothing, but nothing on earth could ever disturb them, short of world chaos.

SO—YOU DECIDE TO MAKE A CALL TO SOMEONE ELSE

You lift the receiver, which activates the hook switch (A), and that action sends some switches into spasms at central. This time, however, you hear that familiar dial tone, which lets you know your two lines are intact and that appropriate voltages are floating along your wires waiting for work. If you have a rotary phone, you'll begin dialing and the mini-switch inside the handset will click the voltages *off* and *on* in accord with the numbers you dial. The pushbutton phone, however, will have cranked up its pad (G) to start generating seven tones through a crystal-controlled oscillator circuit (H) and frequency generator (I).

Each numbered button you push squirts a pair of frequency tones back through the wires, around the induction coils in and out of other parts, then back to your central office.

As fast as the tones are received, they're sorted.

The relay at central says, "Hey, here's a *three* and a *four* and, wow, a *nine*. That's the central office downtown. Go, baby, go!"

And instantly, that prefix lands in its own area station, waiting for you to tell it which of the 9,999 available numbers in that 349 area you're going to pushbutton next.

The whole rigamarole is repeated hundreds of millions of times each day.

If you'd like a little exercise in creative thinking, just imagine what the whole world would be like if suddenly, say in the very next minute, every telephone would vanish. Think of the incredible possibilities that would occur in political, business, domestic, and family affairs. Without those two phone lines from point to point, life as we know it would become almost insufferable within a matter of hours.

EXPLORING YOUR ANSWERING MACHINE

Don't.

No matter whose machine you buy, your chances of taking it apart and giving it any restoration service are very unlikely. There are simply too many multifunction relays, diodes, transistors, mos-fets, zeners, flip-flops, and other such neat technical names for any real person to cope with. Expert technicians despise them. They have inner workings that only their manufacturers can love.

They should run along quite happily with routine care.

If, however, you don't follow your owner's handbook and carry out the regular rituals of dusting the machines, cleaning up the recording heads as the manufacturer describes the process, et cetera, you'll soon own trash instead of treasure.

LEARNING PHONE BIZ

If you really want to learn a lot about your area's phone company, read the vitally important data presented at the front and back ends of your telephone directory. Usually both the white pages and yellow pages are crammed with interesting reading about your system and how it purports to work.

THE NUMBERS GAME

Surely you've noticed the ever-increasing number of free calls you can make along 8oo lines.

800

This prefix for the WATS (Wide Area Telecommunications Service) enables you to call toll-free to hundreds of big companies, mail order businesses, and other groups that want you to keep in touch with them. The service is one of Ma Bell's inventions now being peddled by many resellers as well as AT&T.

The buyer of a WATS line will pay about $125 for installation, $50 to initiate the service, followed by a monthly charge of about $30, plus $25 (approximately) for each fifteen hours of use per month. The buyer can select markets—"rings" of his/her choosing, from 1 (fairly local) to 5 (the U.S. mainland) or 6 (with Puerto Rico, the Virgin Islands, Alaska, and Hawaii).

If you suspect a company might have an 800 number for your areas, call 800 info—dial 1-800-555-1212. The operator will need to know your own area code first before being able to look up your request because of the exquisite selection process that Ma Bell's engineers worked out in setting up the system. And you can buy an 800 telephone book for about $15.

900

The 900 series of numbers is a very special program. Ma Bell uses it to produce direct revenue. Her once-upon-a-time "owned and operated" locals can get into it. It's the line for special occasions such as listening in on the astronauts when they're up in their capsules. It often costs you about 50 cents a minute to listen in on their chitchat. But aren't you impressed we can have such service?

911

Almost worldwide, 911 is a recognized emergency number. New York was one of the first big-city markets for 911 and there were delays in using it to get through to police and fire companies for paramedics or smoke-eaters. It's working better, week by week.

Just never, ever *test* it by dialing. The calling numbers are known instantly and the judge will award you a room with no view, and no telephone, for thirty days, first offense for any misuse. The Los Angeles system took almost a decade to "debug" because of the vast territory that had to be covered. Currently 911 is limited in its coverage outside the big-city areas.

976

This prefix, 976, is becoming the true-boom business when compared to, say, "cellular." Hundreds of entrepreneurs are buying into the prefix from their local companies to produce and supply everything on recorded tape loops that go "round the clock" dispensing a couple of minutes of news, some clean jokes, dirty jokes, news for gays, updates on what the soap operas did today, even bulletins on national heroes, like Michael Jackson, the singer, where he is and what he's doing *now*.

It all depends on the number you call after the 976 prefix. In many cases the phone company supplies the service, directly. Your local operating company might *lease you* a 976 number, if you have an attractive offering. Such local calls will cost you from 25 cents to $3. The phone company gets a share of the profits, and the operator of the service gets a share, as does the producer of the tape, if it's something that needs regular updating. Pacific Bell, which covers much of Los Angeles and San Francisco, earns more than a quarter million dollars a week from people dialing the 976 numbers advertised for sports scores, weather, TV topics, etc. One small company supplying the tapes to New Jersey Bell Telephone grossed a half million dollars supplying only nine programs for a year.

THE COIN BOX STORY

In recent years, the cost of making a call from a coin box on the street has leaped from a nickel to as much as fifty cents just to get a local call. There's a major effort being made to make coin phone service available without a coin. Many big cities will install the system, starting in 1985. You find yourself broke, robbed, or coinless. There'll be a number that will work *free* from all coin boxes. It'll be different from city to city. Check with your local phone company to see if such service is yet available in your area. Make a note of it. You may need it someday.

THE CALLING CARD

If you pay for a telephone at home, chances are good that the local phone company will provide you, for the asking, a "charge card" for use as you go about your affairs in the world. Any call you make from any phone will be charged against your home number if you use it. Obviously, the phone company might politely refuse you such a card if you have an abysmal record of paying your bills or bouncing checks. But a telephone charge card is the one card you might need first and foremost—never leave home without one.

PHONES WITH PICTURE TUBES

Surely you've been saturated with the TV promotion that Ma Bell is giving her new coin-operated phones with a built-in TV screen. It'll give you instructions about making calls, toll charges to certain points, and other advisories that will eliminate human beings at their operations centers. And, of course, it's a subliminal preparation for a return of the "picturefone," which has been gathering dust on Ma's shelves for years. You ain't seen nothin' yet, if Ma has her way.

THE COMING BATTLE ON FLAT RATE SERVICE

Since the beginning of telephone service, residences and businesses have been getting bills for one monthly charge for basic service. You paid the same amount whether you used the phone once a week or nonstop, if the calls were local. Exceptions, of course, were seen in coin telephones, long distance, and some measured charges for senior citizens who were allowed one call per day for a low fee.

Watch for coming attractions. Within a couple of years, when phone rates have been pushed to their outer limits, the companies will begin switching over to "usage charges." After paying a basic rate for having the wires run into your house or business, you'll be metered for every call you make. *And you will be charged accordingly. Please* join a consumers protective group!

GETTING THE CALLER'S NUMBER

You know already, I hope, that when you call your operator or business office, the employee knows the number that you're calling from and the customer in whose name that phone is registered. It pops right up on his or her computer screen. You can see how simple it's going to be to switch into usage service, when the right moment arrives! That's another good reason for joining a citizens action group—you can't fight City Hall or the Phone company all by yourself.

PAGERS

A device of immense importance to individuals in dangerous jobs or suffering from physical problems is a single-button gadget that the user slips over the wrist like an armband or over the head like a necklace. It can be pressed just once to activate an emergency call through the nearby remote phone base. Operators will receive the flashing number and call back. If no answer is received or the caller is unable to respond to questions from the central station, police and medical services will be dispatched. Contact your local phone company for information on availability in your area. The companies that run these businesses can also provide other family members with paging beepers to alert them if a family member uses his or her panic button.

TALK PHONES

The first of a whole new series of robot phones has been launched. The earlier versions were not too reliable. You simply call out the name of "Johnny" and your "talk phone" (I'd rather not plug the name of any particular brand, just yet) will dial Johnny's phone number. In fact, if you program your phone a certain way, it'll keep calling Johnny once a minute if the first try produces a busy signal. I love gadgets, but I'm not yet ready for that one. If you haven't seen one in action in your area, just wait a while. New, improved models will be flooding the market very soon.

TELECONFERENCING

If I hadn't heard that one of Ma's Bell's latest innovations was used by a local family to conduct a cheap "family reunion" among members in New York, Chicago, and Los Angeles, I wouldn't include it in this phone book meant for residential users. Businesses are using the device regularly. Groups gather in rooms set up by Ma Bell in different cities. And they can talk back and forth while watching each other. It's not unlike a conference call of yesterday, except there's a picture, too. Big Business finds it can save bundles of money by using teleconferencing instead of sending its executives around to various conferences, for which registration fees, hotel charges, and airline costs shove the bill through the roof.

THE BOTTOM LINE

By virtue of their monopolistic positioning, Bell Telephone companies, like the gas, electric, and metropolitan transit companies, have had to work under the guidelines determined by public utility commissions. These commissions are usually made up of individuals appointed by state governors or lesser elected officials.

When rate hikes have been requested, the PUCs usually schedule hearings at which civilians can converse with utility professionals. But commissioners are dunned and courted by the lawyers and persuaders of utility companies every day and night of every year.

Now that they're all being "deregulated," we are hearing promises that the competitive factors of a "free market" will hold prices in check, but competition alone may not be effective without your participation.

Obviously, it would be unproductive to have several phone companies franchised for every area, because you could then contact only those individuals using the same system. One answer that is proving to be tremendously effective has been to assure phone companies—and other utilities—a way to maintain healthy service at justifiable rates.

CITIZENS' UTILITY BOARDS

People are banding together under the banner of CUBs (Citizens' Utility Boards). The phone companies and big business are bombarding the public utilities commissions, their lawyers seeking special privileges and discounts, etc.

Wherever CUBs have been courageous enough to form up, utility rates have been held down to reasonable levels of increase. Wisconsin's system, which started the process, way back in '82, continues to grow in membership (citizens are asked to pay $6 a year if they can afford it). And they've sent in lawyers of the people to counterattack the lawyers of the phone companies in search of unbelievable increases. Wisconsin's CUB is reported to have beaten the utilities out of more than $100 million of phony increases in its first year of operation.

When you open your next phone bill, electric bill, gas bill, or water bill, don't faint—get on your phone, dial information (even if they charge you for such service, as some companies now do), and track down a consumers' group you can join to keep Ma Bell and her offspring from cleaning out your bank account.

Appendices

APPENDIX A

STEP-BY-STEP INSTALLATION WITHOUT APPROVED CONNECTORS

1 Assemble your tools, mostly a medium-size screwdriver, a sharp knife, some electrical tape (please, no masking tape or cellophane tape, eh?), and, if you can get one, a soldering iron.

2 Use existing wires and terminals wherever possible, leaving the main entry terminal disconnected. Then, if you can't resist, add on your extra wiring from point to point. Your wire simply *must* have two insulated conductors, right?

3 Test your various telephone sets and accessories. Ask a friend for permission to touch the two (or more) connections from all of your gadgets across any dial tone circuit that he or she has at home. The battery test is a good one, but a nice, fat dial tone is much better.

4 With your sharp knife, carefully remove the insulation at all points where you plan to hook up a telephone or accessory. Scratch away all the dirt and corrosion.

5 If you're still going "dirt poor" with pigtail wire ends on your instruments, give them a thorough cleaning, too.

6 By twisting or wrapping or soldering, even *binding* with a finer wire, strive to get a sturdy mechanical connection between one wire of the equipment to one wire of the phone system. Add one of the "continuing" wires to the same position, again striving for a good mechanical as well as electrical bond. Tape the joint snugly.

7 Proceed to hook up the second wire. Usually, if it's a telephone handset and you want it to ring, you'll fasten the yellow and green wires together on one line, the red, by itself, to the other. You can be certain only by testing as discussed on page 50. As before, add on the continuing conductor. Solder the bunch together and tape snugly.

8 At each step in your installation, momentarily connect the two wires at the terminals on the main entry box. If you've paid Ma Bell and she's provided you with a dial tone, you should hear it loud and clear at your newly acquired and wired telephone.

9 Proceed in the same fashion to wire in other phones and accessories, testing each addition as you go by temporarily hooking up and then unfastening the wires at the main terminal.

10 This connect/disconnect process reduces the possibility of feeling a little nip of electricity if someone happens to ring in while you're holding on to the two bare wire ends. Also, it safeguards the entry box if your soldering iron or some other unexpected source zaps out spikes of high voltage.

As mentioned earlier, the ringing voltage, though high, carries very little current. At the central office there's a "ballast," not unlike an electric light bulb, that senses any oddball conditions out there in Phoneland. It instantly reduces the power to prevent any damage to equipment or amateur installers, like us.

Good luck! Enjoy yourself!

APPENDIX B

STEP-BY-STEP INSTALLATION USING APPROVED CONNECTORS

1 Having surveyed your location, you've bought the approved cabling, preferably six-conductor, 22- or 24-gauge plus the wall mount or surface mount terminals for the several locations where you plan to install phones or accessories at a present or future date.

2 No matter whether your equipment is new or used, pre-test all of it in the modular connectors of a friend's telephone service.

3 By this time you'll have decided whether to use existing wiring and terminals and simply "add-on" new cabling or start over from scratch. If practical for you, install the cabling using round-head approved staples and a round-headed staple gun. Call a tool rental shop if you don't wish to buy one.

4 Follow your survey sketch and begin cabling, hiding the wire behind molding, inside walls and under carpeting if you can locate areas of low or zero foot traffic.

5 The most convenient sockets for most amateurs are those that can be wired under screws. Maintain your color coding as you move along from socket to socket. For reassurance, clip your cabling into place at the main entry point, and if the dial tone is on your line, call a friend or use a free service like "Time" to make a call and check your installations.

6 If you've decided to "go the whole distance," the supply department of your local phone company will have sold you their quick-connect/disconnect terminals and the $5 tool which enables you to press the connectors into place without even removing the plastic insulation.

7 With all the working equipment in place, fasten your connections at the main terminal box, looping the wires under the washers and nuts in a clockwise direction.

Now, relax and tell yourself how smart you are!

APPENDIX C

CLEANING AND RENUMBERING PHONES

Telephone instruments usually respond shiny bright to vigorous applications of soap and water applied and scrubbed with a damp sponge. There are plastic polishes that can help scour away scratches and stains.

On rotary dial instruments, the face plate can be removed in order to change the old number. Simply spin the dial clockwise until the 0 fingerhole reaches the fingerstop. Turn it past the stop, usually about one quarter inch. You'll feel it snub up against a lock tab. Now unbend a small paper clip and press the point down through the tiny hole just inside the fingerhole for 0 and press the lock tab down. A hint of additional clockwise turning and the face plate should pop out into your hand. Clean finger path.

Type your new numbers and area code on a card and set it in place behind the face plate, being careful that the numbers will read easily when the plate is back in position.

Lower the face plate gently into position, twisting it slightly counterclockwise if necessary until it snaps back into position.

If the tiny "paper clip hole" isn't apparent on your handset, you may have to dismantle the dial from the inside out.

On pushbutton phones, most face plates can be pried upward gently with a knife or the entire outer shell can be lifted by removing the holding screw in its base. Go gently, please.

APPENDIX D

PHONE BILL INFORMATION

You're interested in the costs of telephone service, aren't you? Your telephone bill may not tell you. Over the years, the practice of "bundling" charges has served to conceal tariffs for this utility.

If your local company doesn't *unbundle* its monthly bills, start hounding the public utilities commission for your area to insist on getting to the facts.

You may discover that your "basic monthly service charge" might be including the basic access (your two connecting lines for dial tone) plus such little nifties as a charge for an arbitrary basic minimum of "free calls," which you may not ever use, plus, perhaps, rental for the wiring in your location, plus, perhaps, an extra tariff because of a pushbutton phone "special line" or buzzers and ding-dongs which have long ceased to be in your system.

An example may be the home where two lines were once brought onto the premises until one was subsequently disconnected. The "access line" charge might have been deleted by the computer but frequently the accessories, such as lights and disconnect switches, are still being charged against the remaining line.

Phone your local business office and get an item-by-item accounting.

And never hesitate to challenge local toll charges and unfamiliar long-distance billings. In other words, do your own unbundling if your local phone company seems unwilling to do it as a regular practice.

APPENDIX E

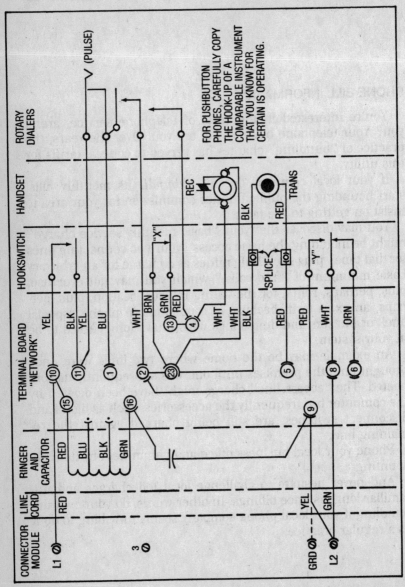

TYPICAL WIRING DIAGRAM TO GUIDE YOU IN CONNECTING MOST (BUT NOT ALL)
TELEPHONE SETS

INDEX

A

AC (alternating current), phone
   bell powered by, 25, 149
Aetna, 140
Allende Gossens, Salvador, 11
alligator clips, 121
Allnet, 41, 138, 139, 140, 142,
   143
Ameritech, 4, 135–36
Ampère, André Marie, 7
amplifiers, 76–77, 98, 104,
   105–6
answering machines, 67–72
   cost of, 67, 70
   early, 68–69
   installation of, 67, 68
   outgoing messages for, 68, 72
   saving long-distance toll
      charges with, 81
   troubles with, 71–72, 152
   used, 71
   with voice-recognition feature,
      100
apartments, locating incoming
   wires in, 124–25
appliances, remote control of,
   106–8
ARGO, 95, 138
AT&T (American Telephone and
Telegraph Company), 1–5,
   10–15
after divestiture, 3, 12–15
founding of, 10
Justice Department vs., 2–3,
   12, 89
long distance services of,
   137–39, 142, 143, 144
Long Lines Division of, 10, 11,
   12
1956 Consent Decree restric-
   tions on, 2
Western Electric division of,
   1, 3, 11, 12, 41, 83
automatic dialers, 42, 45
   with amplifiers, 76–77
   bill-paying services and, 80–81
   with built-in telephones, 77,
      78
   capacity of, 75–76
   good reasons for, 73
   long-distance services and,
      73–74, 75
   with multiline systems, 78
   portable, 97
   used, 78
Automatic Electric, 83
automatic redialers, 42, 45, 75,
   77